CASTLE STREET CAFÉ
COOKBOOK

CASTLE STREET CAFÉ
COOKBOOK

Michael Ballon

G

GADD & COMPANY PUBLISHERS, INC.

Front cover photo and author photo: Michael Lavin Flower © 2007
Cover and book design: Rachel Kaufman

Gadd & Company Publishers, Inc.
An Independent Division of The North River Press Publishing Corporation
292 Main Street
Great Barrington, MA 01230
(413) 528-8895
Visit our website at www.gaddbooks.com

Printed in the United States of America
ISBN: 978-0-9774053-5-0

ACKNOWLEDGMENTS

My career began in my mother's kitchen. In an era of canned vegetables and 1950s convenience foods, it was my very good fortune to have a mother who valued having her own garden and preparing home-cooked meals every day. At an early age, I learned to shuck fresh corn, cut apples for homemade applesauce, and help my mother make her signature raspberry jam. (Of course, one of the fringe benefits of helping out in the kitchen was being able to lick the batter off the mixer when she made a homemade cake.)

I also got an early appreciation for how tough food critics can be as I saw my mother withstand the comments of her hypercritical family. This served me well once I got to New York City, where a restaurant critic's comment that the ice cream we served "seemed to be delicious" might otherwise have been puzzling.

My years in New York gave me the opportunity to work with many talented, and often unheralded chefs who generously shared their techniques, as well as the recipes learned from their own mothers. But my enjoyment and love of food really began at home, in a family that always ate well, took food very seriously, and derived enormous pleasure from a home-cooked meal. For this, I am grateful to my mother.

I am also indebted to the dedicated and loyal employees of the Café, without whom this book would not have been possible. Among the more gratifying comments we hear from our customers is that they feel at home at the Café. My staff's integrity and hard work are evident every day and it is their efforts that make our guests feel welcome and well fed.

Michael Ballon
Chef/Proprietor
Castle Street Café

CONTENTS

SOUPS

SALADS

VEGETABLES

PASTA

SEAFOOD

Saffron Shellfish Sampler • 72

Calamari in Garlic Sauce • 73

Sautéed Red Snapper Niçoise • 74

Grilled Swordfish with Black
Olive and Tomato Salsa • 75

Almond Crusted Brook Trout
With Ginger Orange Sauce • 76

Walnut Crusted Salmon with
Arugula, Orange and Shaved Fennel • 77

Shad Roe with Bacon and Onions • 78

Brook Trout Stuffed
with Mushrooms • 80

Fried Shrimp Dumplings • 83

Halibut with Fresh Tarragon,
Mushroom, and Tomato • 84

Sea Scallops with Turnip Greens • 85

Striped Bass with Shaved
Fennel and Pernod • 86

Striped Bass with Wilted Spinach • 87

Sautéed Salmon with Asparagus and
Saffron Sauce • 88

Cedar Planked Salmon with
Dijon Maple Glaze • 89

Pan Seared Salmon with
Autumn Vegetables • 90

Salmon with Braised Beets • 92

Roasted Salmon with
Roasted Root Vegetables • 94

Sautéed Shrimp with
Angel Hair Pasta, Garlic Sauce • 95

Vegetable Crusted Filet of Sole • 96

Sea Scallops with McCoun
Apples and Coconut Milk • 97

Sea Scallops in Lemongrass Broth • 98

POULTRY

Breast of Chicken with Braised Savoy Cabbage, Mushrooms and Balsamic Glaze • 100

Roast Chicken • 101

Sesame Crusted Chicken Breast with Braised Bok Choy and Ginger Sauce • 102

Breast of Chicken Poached in Plastic Wrap • 104

Breast of Chicken Stuffed with Spinach and Portabella Mushrooms • 106

Breast of Chicken Stuffed with Berkshire Blue, Wrapped with Prosciutto and Sage, Roasted Fig Sauce • 108

Chicken in Sweet Vermouth • 110

Breast of Chicken with Fava Beans • 112

Grilled Cornish Game Hen in Lemon, Fennel and Garlic • 114

Breast of Duck with Black Currants, Braised Apples and Pears • 115

Pan Fried Quail Stuffed with Couscous and Pine Nuts • 116

Warm Duck Salad with Crispy Noodles and Cashews • 118

Breast of Duck with Braised Red Cabbage and Bacon • 120

Sautéed Pheasant with Chanterelles • 122

Apple Walnut Turkey Stuffing • 124

MEAT

Pot Roast • 126

Veal Scaloppini with Lavender • 127

Pork Loin Stuffed with Apricots • 128

Grilled Pork Chops with Crushed Cumin Seeds • 130

Pork Tenderloin with Black-Eyed Peas, Roasted Garlic Sauce • 131

Roast Leg of Lamb • 132

Lamb "Scaloppini" with Roasted Eggplant • 133

Cassoulet of Lamb • 135

Steak au Poivre • 136

Meatloaf • 137

Balsamic and Rosemary Marinated Filet Mignon • 138

Braised Short Ribs • 139

Sautéed Veal Chops with Wild Ramps • 141

CASTLE STREET CAFÉ COOKBOOK

INTRODUCTION

As a professional chef and someone who writes recipes on a regular basis, I am frequently asked for recipes for various dishes. I am happy to provide these, and indeed my website includes a recipe with photos that changes every two weeks. At the same time, it's important to recognize the limitations of recipes, and the importance of technique.

Our intrigue usually begins because we taste something someone else has made that we'd like to recreate, or when looking through a magazine and some recipe or photo strikes our attention. Perhaps you have dined out and seen or tasted something you'd like to try and figure out how to make. When preparing a recipe for the first time, it's always a sound idea to follow the directions exactly, just to see what the result will be. You need a base from which to begin, before you start taking liberties and following your own inspiration. This is particularly true in the realm of baking, where modifying recipes is far more likely to yield unsuccessful results than soups, sauces and other forms of cooking.

Nonetheless, I also caution against following recipes slavishly and ignoring your own judgment and sense of taste. You are ultimately cooking for yourself and your sense of taste, and it is important to know your own palate, and to follow its desires. Some modifications are simple and less risky. Not a fan of spicy food? It's easy to eliminate the hot chilies and crushed red pepper from some international dishes, yet still retain the essential flavor. Curry does not necessarily have to cause sweat to break out on your forehead. Do you have children who don't eat nuts or raisins? Most baked goods that call for these can still be made without them, even if the results are not as tasty as with them. Desserts that taste too sweet can usually be made with less sugar.

Many times a recipe contains a kernel of an idea, or a combination of flavors or seasonings that can be applied to other ingredients to make a dish more to your liking. For example, the essence of many Mediterranean seafood recipes is the classic combination of garlic, tomato, saffron and fennel with shellfish. But if you are allergic to shellfish or just plain squeamish about eating things with tentacles, the same flavor combinations can be combined quite successfully with salmon or flatfish. The essence of Thai and Vietnamese cuisine is the vibrant combination of mint, basil, ginger, garlic and cilantro. You can use these flavors with just about any main ingredient, depending on whether you are a vegetarian, meat, or fish eater. Keeping records of your recipe changes is critical if you want to remember a year or two from now how you made something.

Those watching their diet and intake of fat and cholesterol are always looking for ways to modify recipes to suit their particular diet. Fat, sugar and butter may be reduced or eliminated from various dishes, but don't expect a fettuccine Alfredo made with low-fat milk and half the cheese to taste the same as one made with heavy cream and plenty of cheese.

Before you try out anything on unsuspecting dinner guests, it's always wise to taste it yourself. One of the most common mistakes of even professional chefs is the tendency to combine too many things together in the same dish. How many times have you dined out and either eaten or seen listed on the menu something like grilled halibut with poached figs and a vanilla, thyme and Sauternes sauce served over garlic mashed potatoes? The same dish with one or two fewer ingredients would no doubt be better. The virtue of simplicity is sometimes one of the hardest to learn.

Some of the worst excesses of nouvelle cuisine involved inexperienced chefs using trendy ingredients and untried flavor combinations in an effort to attract attention and gain notoriety for creativity. There's a reason why black pepper ice cream and smoked salmon served with diced kiwis and pink peppercorns are not part of the general repertoire. There are good reasons why some dishes are classics, and why we keep going back to them.

One of the last refuges of unmotivated or unskilled cooks is the claim they if they only had a kitchen like their favorite restaurant, then they too could whip up delicious gourmet meals. In fact, the equipment required to produce a good meal is astonishingly basic. Countless generations of mothers and grandmothers made do with a simple hearth and no refrigeration at all. My grandmother's Brooklyn tenement kitchen could scarcely accommodate two people, had no marble countertops or electric appliances, and had the tiniest ancient stove, yet nonetheless she managed to produce some very memorable meals. Even today we really don't need much more.

Yes, a reliable stove is nice, but most of us have that. Gas burners are certainly preferable to electric, which allow for temperatures to be adjusted more quickly. Convection ovens are nice for baking, as they distribute heat more evenly, but they're not a requirement. Unless one's oven temperature is wildly inaccurate, it's most likely more than sufficient to prepare a good meal.

A couple of basic sauté pans and saucepots are required. There are those who prefer stainless steel and eschew aluminum, but stainless steel pots burn very easily. Copper is both heavy and expensive, and tarnishes easily. Those perfectly polished copper pots seen hanging from a rack in some home kitchens are the ones probably never actually used. Particularly for making sauces and soups, I find heavy bottomed aluminum like Calphalon or All-Clad to be the best. Teflon is unnecessary for just about everything. A couple of flat sheet pans are handy for cookies and other baking.

It is my experience that among the items least likely to be found in many home kitchens is a decent sharp knife. Few things are more frustrating than trying to prepare a meal with a dull knife. Most people will want stainless steel knives in part because they are stainless, and they are certainly a good choice. High carbon knives, which do stain and thus require more care, hold an edge better. There are some extraordinarily good, but quite expensive, Japanese carbon knives on the market today. A basic chef knife, a smaller boning knife, a small vegetable knife and a serrated knife are all that is really required.

There are two items of modern convenience that are very handy to have for anyone who cooks a lot. A food processor for puréeing and chopping food has countless uses. I wouldn't even want to try and count the number of times a day I put something into the bowl of mine at the café. The Cuisinart and Robot Coupe brands are the standards, but many less-expensive models can be purchased that are certainly adequate.

Anyone who bakes regularly will find a KitchenAid mixer almost indispensable. Yes, grandmothers made cakes and cookies before there were electric mixers, but it sure is a lot easier with a power mixer. Frequent bakers will also find that parchment paper makes it much easier and faster to clean up, as well as preventing baked goods from sticking.

It's always nice to have an attractive set of plates, silverware and glasses to serve a meal, but if the food and wine are delicious, what's on the plate and in the glass will be noticed much more than the plate and glass itself.

SOUPS

WILD MUSHROOM SOUP
Serves 4

The following recipe for mushroom soup is made with chicken broth and a variety of different mushrooms, and is a long way from the thick creamy out-of-a-can versions eaten in our childhood. You can purchase a variety of dried mushrooms at specialty stores, and these need only be soaked in boiling water for about 30 minutes to reconstitute. Save some of the liquid the dried mushrooms soak in—it contains a lot of mushroom flavor.

1 onion, peeled and sliced

vegetable oil

½ pound white button mushrooms

¼ pound fresh shiitake mushrooms

½ teaspoon minced garlic

2 ounces dried mushrooms, reconstituted (morels, porcini, shiitake)

1 quart chicken stock

pinch dry basil

pinch dry thyme

2 tablespoons flour

splash soy sauce

splash sherry

minced scallions

salt and pepper to taste

1. In a heavy bottomed saucepot, brown the onions in a little vegetable oil. Add the button and shiitake mushrooms, and stir well.

2 Add the garlic and herbs, and then the flour, and stir well, to mix in the flour.

3. Add the chicken stock and reconstituted mushrooms, and stir well.

4. Let simmer for 20 minutes. Season with salt and pepper, and soy sauce and sherry.

5. Garnish with minced scallions. Serve hot.

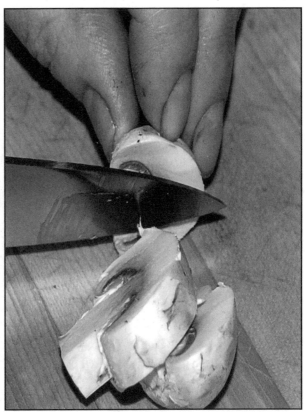

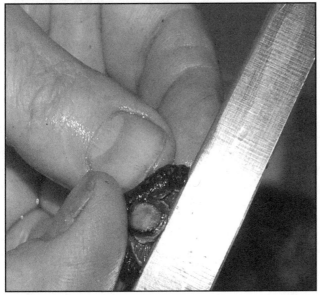

A combination of both fresh and dried mushrooms is best for this soup. Good quality dried mushrooms include a mix of shiitake, morels and porcini. The stems of both fresh and dried shiitakes must be removed, but the stems of button mushrooms may be used.

BLACK BEAN SOUP
Serves 4-6

Few things warm the soul better than a hearty bean soup. Black bean soup is one of my favorites, and the addition of a few crushed red pepper flakes just adds to the warming effects. A generous splash of sherry adds both flavor and smoothness. No meat or stock is required to make this satisfying soup.

1. Soak the beans overnight in water. Drain the soaking liquid, cover the beans with fresh water, and simmer the beans until soft, about 1½ hours. When soft, drain the beans and discard the liquid.

2. In a heavy bottomed saucepot, brown the onion in a little vegetable oil, and add the garlic, cumin, and crushed red pepper flakes.

3. Add cooked beans, and tomatoes, and about 1 quart water. Let simmer for 30 minutes.

4. Purée the liquid in a food processor.

5. Return the purée to the saucepot, taste for salt and pepper, and add the sherry just before serving. Garnish with minced red onions.

1 pound dry black beans

1 Spanish onion, peeled and sliced

vegetable oil

1 tablespoon minced fresh garlic

½ teaspoon ground cumin

½ teaspoon crushed red pepper flakes (optional)

1 quart peeled diced tomatoes

½ cup cream sherry

salt and pepper to taste

minced red onion

SUMMER SQUASH AND TOMATO SOUP

Serves 4

By the end of the summer there is usually a surplus of summer squash and zucchini in the garden, including those that have escaped picking and grown a little too large. The larger ones can be used for soup, combined with some of the bruised and blemished tomatoes. It's one of the last hurrahs of summer, so enjoy.

3 yellow summer squash

1 onion, peeled and diced

olive oil

1 teaspoon minced garlic

pinch fresh basil and thyme

3 cups tomatoes, peeled and seeded

splash sherry

¼ cup Parmesan cheese

1. If the squash are quite large, cut into quarters lengthwise, and remove the large seeds.

2. In a heavy bottomed saucepot, brown the onions in a little olive oil, and then add the squash, basil and thyme, and let brown for 2 minutes.

3. Add the garlic and peeled tomatoes, and simmer for about 20 minutes.

4 Purée the soup in a food processor.

5. Reheat the puréed soup, add the sherry and Parmesan cheese, season with salt and pepper, and serve hot.

POTATO LEEK SOUP WITH CARAWAY

Serves 4

Leeks are among the vegetables that Americans too frequently ignore, which is a shame because they have a delicious and subtle flavor. Part of the onion family, which includes garlic, scallions, and chives, leeks are perhaps the mildest. One of the classic uses of leeks is in a soup made with potatoes. Make sure you wash the leaves well, as the interiors of the leeks tend to be filled with dirt and sand. While many people discard the green top and only use the white bottom, the whole leek is edible. The addition of caraway seeds to the puréed soup adds a very distinctive flavor, as well as some texture. This soup can be made without using any cream, but the addition of the cream makes the soup taste richer.

1 bunch leeks

2 Yukon Gold potatoes

butter or oil

1 Spanish onion

1 quart chicken stock

1 cup heavy cream

salt and pepper

splash sherry

1 bunch scallion, minced

2 tablespoons caraway seeds

1. Wash the leeks carefully to remove any dirt, and then slice into small pieces.

2. Peel and dice the potatoes.

3. In a heavy-bottomed saucepot, lightly brown the onions in a little butter or oil, and add the chopped leeks and potatoes, a pinch of salt, and cover with the chicken stock.

4. Simmer for about 20 minutes, and then purée in a food processor.

5. Return the soup to the pot, add the cream, caraway seeds, and sherry, and taste for salt and pepper. Serve hot.

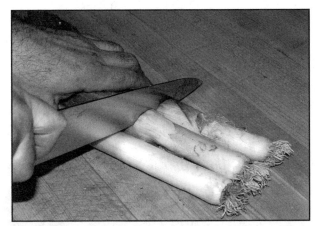

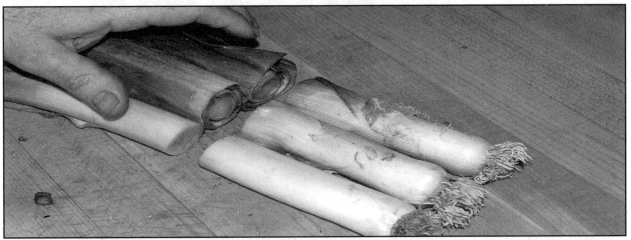

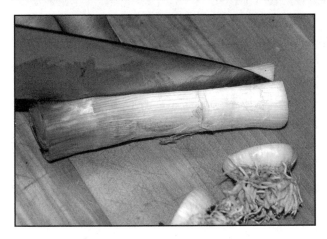

SAFFRON OYSTER BISQUE
Serves 8

Oysters are difficult to serve at home for the average home cook, because opening oysters is a difficult skill, and even experienced oyster shuckers sometimes cut their hands. So for those who want to serve oysters, I offer the following recipe for saffron oyster bisque. The shucked oysters can be purchased from your fish dealer. It can be prepared in advance.

2 quarts fish stock:

flatfish bones

1 onion, sliced

1 carrot, sliced

1 rib celery, sliced

bay leaf

peppercorns

Bisque:

1 Spanish onion, sliced

oil or butter

1 carrot, diced

2 ribs celery, diced

2 tablespoons flour

2 pounds shucked oysters

pinch saffron

2 cups heavy cream

splash sherry

1. To make the fish stock, obtain some flatfish bones from your fish dealer, cover them with cold water. Add a sliced onion, carrot, celery, bay leaf and peppercorns, and bring to a boil, and then let simmer over low heat for 20 minutes. Strain the liquid, and discard the bones.

2. In a heavy-bottomed saucepan, heat a little oil or butter, and brown the onion. Add the celery and carrot, and continue to lightly brown while stirring.

3. Add the flour, mix well, and then add in the fish stock and the saffron. Add the shucked oysters and cream, and simmer over moderate heat for about 20 minutes. Taste for salt and pepper, add the sherry, and serve hot.

TUSCAN BEAN SOUP

Serves 6-8

Bone-chilling weather is the perfect time to serve hearty winter soups. The following recipe for Tuscan Bean Soup is the kind that when served with some great bread is practically a meal in itself. It can easily be made as a vegetarian dish, although the addition of smoked bacon or ham hocks adds another dimension. Purée-ing most of the beans makes for a thick soup, but it's also nice to reserve some of the beans and leave them whole. A thin shaving of fresh Parmesan cheese makes for an elegant garnish.

1. Soak the beans in water overnight, or for at least 12 hours.

2. Cover the beans with water, add a bay leaf, and simmer for about 2 hours, until soft.

3. Purée ¾ of the beans in a food processor.

4. In a heavy bottomed saucepot, brown the bacon until crisp, add the onion, and sauté on medium heat until golden brown, and then add the carrot.

5. Add the garlic and rosemary, the bean purée, as well as the remaining whole beans, and the tomatoes.

6. Add enough water to bring to the proper consistency, and let simmer 30 minutes.

7. Add the scallions, parsley, and sherry, and whisk in the grated Parmesan cheese.

8. Serve hot, with a garnish of shaved Parmesan cheese. (Use a vegetable peeler to shave thin slices off a block of Parmesan cheese.)

1 pound dry white beans (cannelini or Great Northern)

¼ pound smoked bacon (optional)

1 Spanish onion, thinly sliced

1 carrot

1 teaspoon minced garlic

6 ounces peeled diced tomatoes

1 bunch scallion, minced

3 tablespoons minced parsley

pinch fresh rosemary

1 bay leaf

½ cup grated Parmesan cheese

Parmesan cheese for garnish

splash sherry

9

BUTTERNUT SQUASH SOUP
Serves 6

One of the few consolations that summer is over is the arrival of autumn squash. Because they are among the easiest to peel, butternut is my favorite for use in soup. The squash flavor is so delicate that it would be overpowered by using chicken stock, and this is best prepared just with water.

1 butternut squash

2 cups water

½ teaspoon ground cinnamon

¼ teaspoon nutmeg

1 tablespoon grated fresh ginger

½ cup brown sugar (optional)

1 cup heavy cream

salt

1. Peel the squash using a vegetable peeler. Cut the squash in half lengthwise, and scoop out and remove the seeds.

2. Cut the squash into small chunks.

3. In a small pot, add the water, the spices, ginger and brown sugar, if desired, and simmer for about 30 minutes until soft.

4. Purée the cooked squash in a food processor, and pour the purée back into the saucepot.

5. Add the cream, and if the soup is too thick, add more water. Taste for salt, and serve hot.

Spinach soup is one of those things that you simply have to make yourself, because there isn't anything in a can remotely similar to the real thing. There are several keys to making this soup: not overcooking the spinach; using potatoes to help thicken the broth; and puréeing the soup in a blender, as opposed to a food processor. The end result should be a brilliant green color.

1. In a medium-sized pot lightly brown the onions in a little vegetable oil, and season with salt and pepper.

2. Add the cubed potatoes and fresh thyme, and the stock. Cover the pot, and simmer gently about 20 minutes until the potatoes are soft.

3. Take the pot off the stove, and add the spinach directly into the pot, stirring well so the spinach cooks in the hot broth. Be careful to leave the spinach in the hot broth for only about 5 minutes, before transferring the soup to a blender to purée.

4. Purée the soup in a blender in small batches. (A blender yields a much finer purée then a food processor.)

5. Return the purée to the soup pot, add the sherry, and cream. Taste for salt and pepper, and serve hot.

1 large onion, thinly sliced

vegetable oil

2 potatoes, peeled and diced in cubes

1 teaspoon minced fresh thyme

1 quart chicken stock

1 pound cleaned spinach

splash sherry

salt and pepper

1 cup heavy cream (optional)

LOBSTER BISQUE
Serve 4-6

Most people think of eating lobster in the summerime, but lobster bisque is most appealing in cold weather. The soup is made not with the lobster meat. As with making stock, the flavor doesn't come from the meat or flesh, but from the bones or shells. Fortunately your fish purveyor sells lobster shells or carcasses, which have been cleaned of their meat, and these are ideal for making bisque. Steeped in some cream and tomato, they make for a very flavorful soup. The key to extracting all the flavor from the shells is placing them in a mixing bowl with a paddle attachment, and then crushing the shells to release more flavor.

vegetable oil

1 Spanish onion, thinly sliced

1 carrot, finely diced

2 ribs celery, diced

2 lobster shells or bodies

1 cup diced peeled tomatoes

½ cup tomato paste

2 bay leaves

1 teaspoon minced fresh tarragon (or dry)

4 cups heavy cream

⅓ cup sherry

1. In a medium-sized soup pot, lightly brown the carrots, celery, and onions in a little oil. Add the lobster shells, the tomatoes and tomato paste, bay leaves, tarragon and cream.

2. Bring to soft boil, and then turn down the flame and simmer for 20 minutes.

3. Remove the lobster shells from the pot, and place in the bowl of an electric mixer, with the paddle attachment. Turn on low speed and process until the shells become broken and pulverized.

4. Return the ground shells to the stock, and simmer for another 20 minutes.

5. Strain the soup, removing the shells and vegetables. Add the sherry, and serve hot.

THAI BROTH FOR SOBA NOODLES

Makes 1 quart

The distinctive taste of Thai cuisine is the result of the blending of many different seasonings. Garlic, ginger, mint, basil, hot chilies, coriander, soy sauce, and fish paste are just some of the seasonings that are combined together in one dish. The following recipe for broth is vegetarian. Chicken or fish stock could certainly be substituted, but the broth is so highly seasoned that it is not essential. If you prefer a slightly thicker broth, a little cornstarch dissolved in cold water can be added at the end. Once the broth is made it can be served over soba noodles with the addition of vegetables and shrimp or scallops to make a filling and delicious main course. Feel free to vary the seasonings to your own taste.

1 Spanish onion, peeled and thinly sliced

1 teaspoon minced ginger

1 teaspoon minced garlic

¼ teaspoon dried hot red pepper flakes

4 cups water

2 tablespoons sesame oil

grated zest of 1 orange

1 bunch mint, finely chopped

1 bunch basil, finely chopped

1 bunch coriander, finely chopped

1 bunch scallions, finely minced

½ cup soy sauce

1. Brown the onion in the sesame oil until golden brown, and then add the ginger, garlic, and red pepper flakes.

2. Stir well, and then add the water and the remaining ingredients.

3. Let simmer for about 15 minutes.

4. To serve, heat up some soba noodles with a variety of vegetables (bok choy, snow peas, broccoli, red peppers, shiitake mushrooms) in the broth, and serve immediately.

WATERMELON AND MANGO SOUP

Serves 6-8

There are days when it is so hot that eating solid food scarcely seems possible. In the heat of summer it sometimes feels like all we need to do is drink liquids. One such quencher is a purée of watermelon and mango, spiked with ginger. The new seedless varieties of watermelon spare you the effort of having to remove seeds. A blender yields a smoother purée than a food processor. Served chilled, this is the perfect treat on a scorching day.

1 seedless watermelon

2 mangoes

1 tablespoon minced ginger

½ cup blueberries

1. Scoop the flesh out of a watermelon, and remove any seeds.

2. Cut the melon into chunks, and purée in a blender with the ginger.

3. Peel the mangoes, and dice the flesh into small chunks, and add to the melon purée.

4. Garnish with blueberries, and serve chilled, with a sprig of mint.

CHILLED CUCUMBER DILL SOUP
Serves 4

Anytime the thermometer gets above 80° is an appropriate time to begin a meal with cold soup. A purée of cucumber can be used either as a sauce or a soup—the addition of a little more stock yields a thinner result, which is suitable for soup; a thicker purée can be used as a sauce for cold poached salmon. A blender always produces a smoother purée than a food processor, but the food processor is acceptable. This recipe calls for sour cream, but low-fat yogurt can be substituted for those trying to eliminate fat. The heavy cream is optional, but obviously makes for a richer soup.

2 cucumbers

¼ red onion

2 tablespoons minced fresh dill

3 tablespoons sour cream

2 cups chicken stock

splash sherry

splash soy sauce

salt to taste

1. Peel the cucumbers, cut them in half, and remove the seeds. Chop them into pieces.

2. Purée the cucumbers, dill, and red onion in a blender or food processor with the sour cream and chicken stock.

3. Add the splash of sherry and soy sauce, taste for salt, and serve chilled, with a sprig of dill on top as garnish.

CHILLED CANTALOUPE AND GINGER SOUP

Serves 4-6

The following truism about life is especially true about food: the best things in life are simple. And yet the simplest things can also be the hardest to do. There are really only three ingredients in the following recipe for chilled cantaloupe soup, which means that the key ingredient, the cantaloupe, must be of the highest quality. Nothing but the juiciest and ripest melons should be used in this recipe, which means that it can only be made in the summer. The same is true for the orange juice; fresh squeezed makes all the difference in the world. The clean taste of the ginger is refreshing, and the soup is delicate and light.

2 large ripe cantaloupes

1 tablespoon minced fresh ginger

3 cups fresh orange juice

fresh mint

1. Cut the melons in half, remove the seeds, and scoop out the flesh.

2. Cut into chunks.

3. Purée the melons and ginger in a blender. (A blender works better than a food processor.)

4. Add the orange juice, and chill.

5. Serve with a sprig of fresh mint.

During the two months of the year when it is possible to buy real locally raised vine ripe tomatoes, it is time to make gazpacho. It's almost always possible to buy bruised or slightly blemished tomatoes at a discount, and bargain seekers know that these are ideal for making sauce, and for use in soup. While you don't want to buy a rotten or decomposing tomato, one with cracked skin or a small blemish that can be easily removed is ideal for cooking. It's simple to blanch and peel a tomato—simply remove the core with a paring knife, drop in boiling water for 15 seconds, and then plunge into ice water. The skin then easily peels off, and you're ready to make soup or sauce. It's the basis of the following recipe for that summer classic—gazpacho. Bon appétit!

4 large ripe tomatoes

1 cucumber, peeled and seeded

½ small red onion

½ teaspoon minced garlic

1 bunch scallion, minced

1 tablespoon finely chopped basil

1 tablespoon finely chopped parsley

3 tablespoons extra virgin olive oil

2 tablespoons balsamic vinegar

6 ounces V-8 or tomato juice

splash Tabasco or hot sauce to taste

1. Remove the cores of the tomatoes, score the bottom of the tomatoes with an "X" mark, drop into boiling water for 15 seconds, then plunge into ice water.

2. Peel the skin off, and cut the tomatoes in half, and squeeze out the seeds.

3. Place the tomatoes, cucumber, red onion, and garlic in a blender or food processor, and purée.

4. Add the remaining ingredients, and taste for salt and pepper. Serve well chilled, with some minced scallion or herbs on top.

SALAD

Beet, Endive and Walnut Salad • 20

Scallop and Spinach Salad • 22

Spinach Salad with Crottin • 23

Roasted Barley Salad • 24

Mango and Mint Salad • 25

Mesclun and Jicama Salad • 26

Warm Chicken Salad with
Balsamic Vinaigrette • 27

Wild Rice Salad • 28

Grilled Shrimp Caesar Salad • 29

Warm Salad of Frisée and Bacon • 30

Chilled Seafood Salad • 31

BEET, ENDIVE, AND WALNUT SALAD WITH WALNUT VINAIGRETTE

Serves 4

During the colder months, a salad of beets and endive is more substantial salad than mere greens, and is a classic combination. As the doctors from Canyon Ranch point out in their book *Ultra Prevention*, it is the brightly colored vegetables that are the healthiest, and beets are nothing if not colorful. They are particularly delicious with vinaigrette made from walnut oil.

4 large beets

½ cup walnuts

½ cup walnut oil

2 tablespoons rice wine vinegar

2 heads Belgian endive

1. Place the beets in a small saucepot, cover with water, add a pinch of salt, and bring to a boil.

2. Let the beets simmer for about 20 minutes. They are done when a paring knife can be easily inserted into the center.

3. When cooked, drain and cool.

4. Peel off and discard the outer skin, which comes off by rubbing the cooked beets with a kitchen towel.

5. Dice the beets in uniform pieces, and place in a mixing bowl

6. Add the oil and vinegar to the bowl and toss well.

7. Cut off the bottoms of the endive, separate the leaves, and fan out the leaves around the center of 4 plates.

8. Mound the beets into piles in the center of each plate.

9. Top with walnuts, and serve immediately

SCALLOP AND SPINACH SALAD

Serves 4

The affinity between lemon and seafood is well established. The combination of orange and seafood is also delicious. The following salad of slightly wilted spinach with sautéed scallops combines sections of orange with a dressing made from orange zest and juice to make a light refreshing dish. Be careful cooking the spinach, as too much cooking will yield a wet, overcooked mass of greens.

Dressing:

zest of 1 orange

juice of 1 orange

⅓ cup rice wine vinegar

1 teaspoon Dijon mustard

1 cup olive oil

2 pounds sea scallops

1 red pepper, thinly sliced

2 portabella mushroom caps thinly sliced

½ red onion, thinly sliced

2 pounds cleaned spinach, stems removed

2 oranges, sliced into sections, skin and pith removed

1. To make the dressing, combine the zest and juice of the orange with the vinegar and mustard. Slowly whisk in the olive oil. Save the body of the orange, and use a small knife to separate the sections, and reserve.

2. In a large skillet, sauté the scallops for about 2 minutes on each side, and then remove them from the pan.

3. Add the red onion slices, red pepper, and mushroom, and sauté for 1 minute.

4. Add the spinach to the skillet, toss and shake well, and then add about ½ cup dressing directly into the pan.

5. Remove the pan from the stove, and continue to toss until the spinach is slightly wilted.

6. Place the spinach mix in the center of 4 plates, and arrange the scallops around the plate. Drizzle a little additional dressing on top. Garnish with the reserved orange sections.

SPINACH SALAD WITH CROTTIN

Serves 4

The Berkshire area is blessed with a number of outstanding local cheesemakers who make a wide variety of cow, goat, and sheep milk cheeses. For those who have never tried it and are scared at the prospect of eating sharp-tasting cheese, the mild flavor will be a revelation. It's delicious on a salad of baby spinach.

1. Preheat oven to 350°

2. Toast the almonds in the oven till golden brown, and when cool, chop finely.

3. Press the almonds into the top of the crottin, and warm in the oven for about 2 minutes. The cheese should be slightly warm, but still intact.

4. Toss the spinach with a vinaigrette, and place the almond-crusted crottin on the top. Serve immediately.

3 tablespoons toasted almonds

4 crottins (small goat cheese rounds)

1 pound baby spinach, washed

¾ cup vinaigrette

ROASTED BARLEY SALAD
Serves 6-8

For most people barley is a sometimes ingredient in soup, as in mushroom barley or vegetable barley soup. Barely however, is a grain that can stand on its own, like wild rice, couscous, or quinoa. Today it's not uncommon to see barley served as a grain or starch with meat or fish, and it makes a refreshing change from the same old rice or potatoes. The following recipe for barley salad is made by first toasting the grains in the bottom of a saucepot, and then adding a variety or seasonings and minced vegetables to the cooked grain. It makes a great accompaniment to grilled chicken or fish.

1 pound barley

¼ cup dry black currants

¼ cup toasted sunflower or pumpkin seeds

1 red pepper, finely minced

¼ red onion, finely minced

grated zest of 1 orange

½ cup olive oil

¼ cup orange juice

¼ cup rice wine or raspberry vinegar

salt and pepper

1. In a heavy bottomed saucepot, toast the barley in a little bit of oil over moderate heat for about 3 minutes.

2. Cover the barley with water, and simmer over moderate heat for about 15 minutes, until soft.

3. Drain the barley well, and rinse under cold water to wash away the excess starch.

4. When cool, combine the barley with the remaining ingredients, mix well, and taste for salt and pepper. Serve cool or at room temperature, with grilled meat or fish.

MANGO AND MINT SALAD
Serves 4

Mangoes and mint make a delicious combination for a chunky salad, which can be enjoyed by itself, or as a condiment with grilled fish and chicken. Even if the weather isn't cooperating, we can at least think spring by enjoying this piece of the tropics. It takes a few minutes to cut up all the ingredients into small pieces, but the result is worth the effort.

1. Cut up the mangoes, tomato, and cucumber into a small dice.

2. Finely chop all the fresh herbs.

3. Combine all the vegetables, fruit, and herbs in a bowl, and toss with the oil and vinegar. Serve immediately.

2 mangoes

1 tomato

1 seedless cucumber

1 red pepper

½ jalapeño

1 bunch fresh mint

½ bunch cilantro

⅓ cup rice wine vinegar

1 cup olive oil

MESCLUN AND JICAMA SALAD

Serves 4

While the days of eating iceberg lettuce are over for many people, some miss the crispness that is simply lacking in the softer greens that make up mesclun lettuce. Oak leaf and mache, while flavorful greens, simply don't have the snappy crispness of iceberg lettuce. One solution to the lack of crispness of mesclun salad is to combine it with some other vegetables, especially jicama. Jicama is a tuber which looks like a potato, and when eaten raw lends a moistness and crunch to salad. The addition of a julienne of jicama, along with some mung beans and thinly sliced seedless cucumber and red pepper adds color and texture to salads, and makes for a sturdy and flavorful base for a seafood or chicken salad.

½ pound mesclun greens

1 jicama, peeled and julienne

1 seedless cucumber,
peeled and sliced

1 red pepper, thinly sliced

1 cup mung bean sprouts

Dressing:

1 cup olive oil

⅓ cup red wine vinegar

1 teaspoon Dijon mustard

½ teaspoon finely chopped ginger

2 tablespoons chopped
roasted peanuts or cashews

1. Wash the mesclun greens and dry carefully.

2. In a large bowl, combine the jicama, red pepper, seedless cucumber and mung beans with the salad greens, and mix well.

3. Combine the dressing ingredients together in a small jar, and shake well. Toss the salad with the dressing, and serve on 4 plates. Top with roasted nuts. Serve alone, or with grilled seafood or poultry.

WARM CHICKEN SALAD, BALSAMIC VINAIGRETTE

Serves 4

It wasn't long ago that chicken salad meant a rich concoction dripping with mayonnaise, but today's diet-conscious eaters demand lighter fare. It's a radically different proposition to place some grilled chicken breasts over some mesclun greens tossed with a vinaigrette. Interesting salad greens are essential, and a good mesclun mix contains a vibrant combination of baby mustard greens, lola rossa, oak leaf lettuces and herbs. An empty jar or bottle makes shaking up a little vinaigrette a quick and simple task. The variations on garnishing this salad are endless: roasted peppers, grilled fennel, shaved Parmesan, or simply great tomatoes all make tasty additions.

4 boneless chicken breasts

1 pound mesclun salad greens, washed and dried

1. Trim any fat off the chicken breasts, and pound them with a meat mallet to flatten them out a little.

2. Grill over high heat, for about 2 minutes on each side.

3. Allow to cool for 2 minutes, then slice the meat into thin strips.

Dressing:

1 teaspoon Dijon mustard

⅓ cup balsamic vinegar

1 cup olive oil

4. To make the dressing, combine the vinegar and mustard in a small jar and shake together well. Then add the olive oil and shake again.

5. Toss the greens with the dressing, and place the strips of meat on top. Make whatever additions you prefer, and serve immediately.

roasted peppers, grilled fennel, tomatoes, if desired

WILD RICE SALAD
Serves 6-8

1 pound cooked
wild rice

1 red pepper,
finely minced

1 carrot, finely
minced

½ head celery,
finely minced

½ cup toasted
almond slivers

½ cup dry black
currants

½ pound red
grapes sliced in half

grated zest of
1 orange

½ cup fresh-
squeezed
orange juice

¼ cup rasp-
berry vinegar

½ cups veg-
etable oil

2 tablespoons
honey

Summer entertaining calls for dishes that can be prepared in advance and don't require a lot of time in the kitchen, yet nonetheless are delicious and will impress guests. Wild rice salad fits the bill on all accounts. It can be made a day or two in advance, is healthy, and makes a great accompaniment to both grilled meat and seafood. The addition of citrus and nuts give it a crisp and vibrant taste, and there is a wide variety of ingredients that may added to the cooked rice. Minced celery, red pepper, diced carrots, dried currants and any of your favorite nuts all add to the mix.

1. To make the rice, cover with water, cook for about 1 hour, drain excess water, and cool.

2. Combine the rice with the remaining ingredients in a bowl, and mix well.

3. Feel free to add a greater variety of nuts (such as pecans or walnuts if you wish), or perhaps minced red onion.

4. Serve chilled or at room temperature.

Caesar Salad remains a timeless classic partly for its crunch. But that doesn't mean it cannot also be updated and augmented with the addition of grilled shrimp. The key is obviously the dressing, and a blender or food processor yields a thick creamy dressing. And the anchovies are always optional.

24 large shrimp, shelled and deveined

juice of 1 lemon

½ teaspoon minced garlic

pinch fresh thyme

1 tablespoon olive oil

Dressing:

⅔ cup red wine vinegar

1 teaspoon Dijon mustard

1 egg yolk

2 cups vegetable oil

½ small red onion

½ teaspoon garlic

¼ cup Parmesan cheese

4 anchovies (optional)

2 heads romaine, washed and cut in pieces

1 cup croutons

1. Marinate the shrimp in the lemon juice, garlic, thyme and olive oil for 15 minutes, and then cook on a hot grill for about 2 minutes on each side.

2. Combine the mustard, red onion, garlic, and vinegar with the yolk in a blender or processor, and purée. Slowly add in the vegetable oil, and when finished, add the cheese. The dressing should be creamy and slightly thick.

3. Toss the romaine and croutons with the dressing, and arrange on 4 plates. Arrange 6 shrimp on each of the plates, and garnish with the anchovy filets. Serve immediately.

WARM SALAD OF FRISÉE
AND BACON

Serves 4

Dressing:

1 egg yolk

1 teaspoon minced shallot

2 tablespoons Dijon mustard

¾ cup red wine vinegar

2 cups soybean oil

salt and pepper

¼ cup cooked bacon lardons

2 heads frisée (curly headed chicory) washed and dried

2 portabella mushrooms, grilled or roasted

¼ cup salad croutons

In this country there isn't a tradition of eating warm salads, but in Europe they are a part of the culinary heritage. Hearty greens like frisée, chicory, or even kale are essential to the dish. Obviously delicate salad greens like leaf lettuces are not sturdy enough to take the heat. The bacon is optional, but traditional. The trick in making these salads is to toss the greens quickly, and to serve them immediately.

1. Prepare a thick Dijon vinaigrette by combining the egg yolk with the minced shallot and mustard. Slowly whisk in the red wine vinegar with the vegetable oil, whisking well between additions. Use only ½ cup for the warm salad, and save the rest for other salads.

CHILLED SEAFOOD SALAD

Serves 4-6

The following recipe for chilled seafood salad is perfect for summer entertaining and dinner outdoors. Shellfish works best for seafood salad, as the fish retains its shape and remains recognizable. This dish can be prepared ahead of time and served with a variety of side dishes, like asparagus vinaigrette, or on a bed of salad greens, to make a complete dinner.

1 pound peeled and deveined shrimp

1 pound sea scallops

½ pound lump crabmeat

Dressing:

1 bunch basil

1 cup olive oil

⅓ cup rice wine vinegar

2 cloves garlic

1 bunch scallions, minced

¼ cup minced red pepper

¼ cup diced red onion

1 ripe tomato, diced

salt and pepper to taste

1. Remove the small side muscle from the scallops, which is chewy and unpleasant to eat.

2. Drop the shrimp and scallops into a large pot of salted water and cook for about 2 minutes, until tender but still firm. Remove the fish from the pot, and plunge in ice water.

3. Drain the cooked shrimp and scallops, and place in a large mixing bowl with the crabmeat.

4. To make the dressing, remove the basil leaves from the stem and wash well. Purée the washed leaves in a blender with the olive oil, garlic, and vinegar.

5. Combine all the diced vegetables with the seafood, add the dressing and mix well. Taste for salt and pepper. Serve chilled, on a bed of greens.

VEGETABLES

WHITE ASPARAGUS AND GOAT CHEESE GRATIN

Serves 4

While most of us are familiar with green asparagus, in Europe the white variety is highly prized. White asparagus is grown completely underground, which keeps the vegetable pale. The flavors are similar, but the white variety is generally milder. Combined with a light goat cheese sauce and gratinéed under a broiler, they make a delicious first course.

1 pound white asparagus

1 teaspoon butter

1 teaspoon flour

1 cup milk

¼ cup soft goat cheese

salt and pepper

4 thin slices Swiss cheese

¼ cup Parmesan cheese

1 tablespoon finely chopped parsley

1 tomato, diced into small cubes

1. Trim the bottoms off the asparagus, and blanch quickly in boiling water. Cool in ice water, and drain well.

2. Melt the butter in a small saucepan, and add the flour to make a thin paste. Whisk in the milk slowly, and stir well as you bring to a boil over moderate heat. The sauce should thicken slightly.

3. Whisk in the goat cheese, stir well and taste for salt and pepper. Set aside and keep warm.

4. Place the asparagus on a heavy broiling pan, cover with the Swiss cheese, and then sprinkle the top with the grated Parmesan cheese.

5. Place under the broiler for about 30 seconds, or until the cheese is golden brown.

6. Spoon out a little of the goat cheese sauce on the bottom of four dinner plates, and divide the gratineed asparagus among the 4 plates. Sprinkle the diced tomato and parsley on top, and serve immediately.

END OF SUMMER CORN SALAD
Serves 6

If by the end of summer you've eaten your share of corn on the cob, you may want to try the following recipe for southwestern corn salad. This recipe is particularly good if you boil come corn and then have leftover cooked ears. Strip the kernels off the cob with a sharp paring knife, and combine the corn with the rest of the ingredients to make a refreshing salad. It's a great accompaniment to grilled meat or fish.

4 cooked ears of corn

1 small red onion, diced

1 bunch scallion, finely chopped

1 red pepper, diced

1 tomato, peeled and diced

½ bunch cilantro, finely chopped

½ teaspoon minced garlic

⅓ cup sherry wine vinegar (red wine or balsamic may be substituted)

1 cup olive oil

salt and pepper

1. Use a small sharp knife to strip the kernels off the ears of corn. Then using a large chef knife, carefully dice the corn into small pieces.

2. Combine the corn with the remaining ingredients in a bowl and toss well. Taste for salt and pepper. Serve with grilled chicken, fish or meat.

ARTICHOKE VINAIGRETTE
Serves 4

It's not obvious when first encountered that artichokes are meant to be eaten, and it no doubt took our ancestors a while to figure that out. When fresh artichokes are available in the markets, and relatively inexpensive, there's no excuse for eating the canned hearts. The process of eating a whole artichoke and pulling off the leaves is a sensual food experience, which while a little messy, is very rewarding. The hairy and spiky choke is located in the center, just above the heart, and must be removed. Timing is everything in cooking artichokes—too long, and they fall apart; too little, and the flesh is too tough to chew. A liberal drenching with your favorite vinaigrette transforms them into a delicious appetizer. For those accustomed to the canned variety, this will be a revelation.

4 artichokes

1 cup vinaigrette dressing

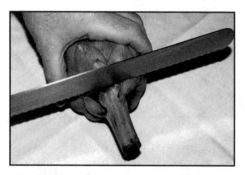

1. Trim the stems off the bottoms of the artichokes so they sit flat on a counter.

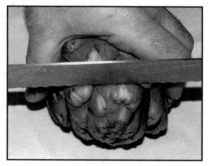

2. Place them on their sides, and using a serrated knife, cut off the top ⅓ of each artichoke, and discard.

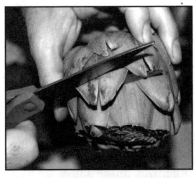

3. Trim the pointy ends of the leaves with a scissors, cutting off the sharp ends.

4. Bring a pot of lightly salted water to a boil, and place the artichokes in it. Make sure they are submerged in the water by placing a small weight, such as a few dishes or a small pan, on top.

5. Cook them for about 20 minutes, and test for doneness by pulling off a leaf from the bottom and chewing on the pulpy end. The leaf should be pleasantly soft when cooked.

6. When finished cooking, carefully remove the artichokes from the pot and submerge in ice water to cool.

7. Drain well. Using a small spoon, dig into the center of the artichoke and remove the inedible choke from the center.

8. Place the artichokes on 4 plates, pull off several of the bottom leaves on each plate, and arrange around the artichoke in the center. Pour the vinaigrette into the center of the artichoke and around the plate, and serve immediately.

MUSHROOM STRUDEL IN PHYLLO PASTRY
Serves 6-8

Phyllo pastry is a thin flaky dough that requires great care to use, but yields a delicious and light pastry. Commonly used in the Mediterranean for savories and sweets, the ultra-thin leaves can be filled with a great variety of ingredients. Phyllo dough can be difficult and frustrating to work with, as the separate leaves of dough sometimes stick together, and patience is required. The following recipe for mushroom strudel makes a great fall dish, which does require both time and care to assemble, but the result is worth the effort.

1 Spanish onion, peeled and sliced

vegetable oil

1 pound domestic button mushrooms

1½ pounds shiitake mushrooms, stems removed

sprig fresh thyme

4 portabella mushrooms

1 package phyllo pastry

½ stick melted unsalted butter

1 bunch scallion, chopped

parchment paper

1. Preheat oven to 400°

2. Cook the onion in a little oil until well browned, and set aside.

3. Slice the mushrooms, and brown in a sauté pan with the fresh thyme. Place the cooked mushrooms in a colander for about 30 minutes, and let the liquid drain out.

4. Place the cooked onions and mushrooms in a food processor, on pulse. Leave the mushrooms a little chunky, and be careful not to over-process.

5. Lay out the leaves of phyllo dough, and brush with the melted butter. Place the mushroom purée on one side of the pastry, and roll up like a jellyroll, brushing the dough with more melted butter along the way.

6. Place on baking sheet lined with parchment paper, and bake for about 25 minutes, until the pastry is crisp and brown on top. Serve warm. Garnish with chopped scallions.

SAUTÉED KALE
Serves 4

In a continuing series of vegetable affirmative action, consider the lowly kale. It's ignored by most people, and probably used as a garnish more often than eaten. It's one of the last vegetables to be harvested from the garden, long after the tomatoes and lettuces of summer are gone. The sturdy leaves must be cooked for quite a long time to render them tender, and a generous amount of bacon and onions helps the cause. Unlike spinach, which wilts in just seconds in a skillet, the kale will hold up to extended cooking. It will be so delicious you might not even know how nutritious it is for you.

2 large bunches of kale

¼ pound slab bacon, cut into cubes

1 Spanish onion, sliced

½ teaspoon minced garlic

1. Trim off the bottom stems of the kale, cut the bunch in half, and wash well.

2. In a large skillet, brown the bacon until it releases some fat into the skillet, and then add the onion. Cook until lightly browned.

3. Add the garlic and kale and stir well.

4. Add about ¼ cup of water to the pan, place a lid on top of the skillet, and allow to cook for between 5-10 minutes over moderate heat.

5. Remove the cover, stir well, and serve with roasted or grilled meat.

ZUCCHINI LATKES

Serves 4-6

At the end of summer it takes creativity to use the surplus of zucchini. Zucchini bread and cake are two ways, and latkes, or zucchini pancakes, is another. They are delicious when fried, but it is necessary to remove some of the water this vegetable contains. The technique involves grating the zucchini, salting them, and covering them with a weight, which draws out the water. By pressing out the excess water, the remaining grated vegetable is firmer and more solid. When fried as a thin pancake, they make delicious eating, especially with a dollop of sour cream on top.

1. Grate the zucchini and onion, either in a food processor, or with an old fashioned 4-sided hand grater.

2. Toss the grated vegetables with the salt, and place in a colander. Place several plates on top of the vegetables to press out the water.

3. Allow the zucchini to drain for about 30 minutes. Remove the plates and press out any additional water by hand.

4. Mix the grated vegetables with the eggs and flour.

5. Heat a skillet with a little vegetable oil, and fry the latkes in hot oil for about 2 minutes on each side. Serve hot, with a dollop of sour cream.

2 zucchini

vegetable oil

1 onion

1 tablespoon kosher salt

3 eggs

1 cup flour

sour cream

STUFFED ACORN SQUASH

Serves 4

Stuffed acorn squash is a classic autumn dish. A combination of apples, walnuts and dried cranberries makes a colorful and seasonal accompaniment to a meal, or even a main course. The squash must first be cut in half and baked for about 40 minutes until soft. Then the stuffing can be added and the dish cooked some more. The sweeter spices, like ginger, cinnamon and nutmeg are traditional, but be careful to avoid adding too much sugar, or it will seem more like dessert than dinner.

2 acorn squash

2 Macintosh apples

2 Granny Smith apples

fresh ginger, minced

1 cup dried cranberries (or dried black currants)

1 cup walnuts

dash cinnamon

butter

brown sugar

1. Preheat oven to 350°

2. Cut the squash in half, and scoop out the seeds.

3. Bake the squash cut side down on a baking pan for about 40 minutes.

4. Core and dice the apples, and sauté briefly in a little butter with the fresh ginger.

5. Combine the dried fruit with the nuts and apples, and stuff the center of the squash.

6. Top the stuffing with a few butter pats, and a sprinkling of brown sugar.

7. Bake for another 20 minutes, and serve hot.

STUFFED ZUCCHINI

With zucchini popping up out of the garden faster than most people can eat them, it's important to come up with new recipes. The larger ones are ideal for stuffing. Cut them in half lengthwise, scoop out some of the seeds, and then stuff and bake. They can be stuffed with a variety of ingredients, including ground meat, but the following recipe is vegetarian, and makes for a delicious meal.

1. Preheat oven to 350°

2. Cut the zucchini in half lengthwise, and scoop out the seeds.

3. In a sauté pan, sauté the onions in a little oil over low heat until golden brown, about 15 minutes.

4. In a separate pan, sauté the mushroom slices in a little olive oil.

5. In a large mixing bowl, combine the sautéed onions, mushrooms, and chopped spinach; add the thyme, basil and garlic. Add the Parmesan cheese, eggs and breadcrumbs, and mix well.

6. Stuff the zucchini with the prepared stuffing, and sprinkle a little additional Parmesan cheese on top.

7. Bake for 20 minutes. Serve with rice pilaf.

4 large zucchini

olive oil

1 Spanish onion, peeled and sliced

1 pound button mushrooms, sliced

8 ounces spinach, washed and chopped

½ teaspoon garlic, minced

1 cup breadcrumbs

fresh thyme and basil, chopped

4 eggs, beaten

1 cup Parmesan cheese

43

ASIAN SLAW
Serves 6-8

1 jicama

1 carrot, peeled

1 red pepper

1 seedless cucumber

Dressing:

1 cup vegetable oil

⅓ cup rice wine vinegar

1 teaspoon Dijon mustard

1 teaspoon minced shallot

½ teaspoon minced or puréed fresh ginger

1 tablespoon Indonesian sweet soy sauce (available in specialty food stores)

¼ pound mesclun greens, washed

¼ pound mung bean sprouts

cashews, chopped

Those looking to inject a little crunch and crispness into their salad greens will enjoy the following recipe for Asian slaw. By mixing the greens with a julienne of jicama, carrot, red pepper, and seedless cucumber, as well as some mung beans, the greens are transformed into a crispy Asian slaw. Jicama is one of the too-ignored vegetables. They look like potatoes, and must be peeled the same way, and they taste like a cross between an apple and a potato. They add a distinctive juiciness and crunch to the following recipe, which can be the basis for a duck or shrimp salad with Asian slaw.

1. Peel the jicama, and cut into thin julienne slices. Do the same with the carrot, red pepper, and cucumber.

2. The dressing can be prepared by hand in a bowl using a whisk, or in a blender. Combine the mustard, shallots, ginger, rice vinegar and soy sauce, and mix well. Slowly add the oil, mixing well after each addition.

3. In a large bowl toss the greens with the mung beans and the julienne vegetables. Toss with the dressing. Serve alone, or as the basis for a salad made of grilled duck, shrimp or poultry. Garnish with chopped cashews.

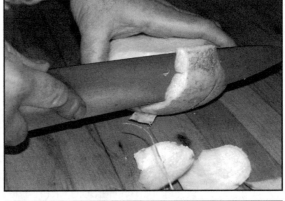

Jicama (pronounced hee-ka-ma) is the root of a perennial legume whose vine may grow to 20 or more feet. The exterior of this globe-shaped tuber is parchment brown, concealing the crisp white flesh within. Grown mostly in Mexico and South America, they are available in the produce section of many markets. Look for heavy, dense roots and smooth skin. Store in a cool, dry place; too much moisture will cause mold.

POTATO GALETTE
Makes 4 Galettes

Some of the best things in life are the simple ones, and the following recipe is as simple as it gets. There are really only two ingredients—potatoes and a little melted butter, but the results are sophisticated and delicious and perfect for special occasions. Potato galettes are thin crispy potato cakes made by slicing potatoes into thin silver-dollar-shaped discs, tossing them with butter, and then forming a hand-sized circle of overlapping slices, which when baked yield a thin cake. The key is slicing the potatoes very thinly, which can be done by hand with a sharp knife and a lot of care, or using a mandolin, which is a vegetable slicer. They make a dramatic presentation on the plate, and are simple to make.

 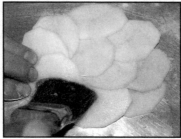 

1. Preheat oven to 375° Slice the potatoes as thinly as possible into round discs.

3 potatoes, peeled

2. Toss the slices with the melted butter and salt and pepper to taste.

2 tablespoons melted butter

salt and pepper

parchment paper

3. Line a baking sheet with parchment paper to prevent the galettes from sticking.

4. Layer the slices into a 4" circle, slightly overlapping each slice.

5. Bake for about 15-20 minutes or until golden brown and crisp. Remove from the pan, and serve hot with grilled fish or meat.

At the end of summer, farmers' markets and your neighbors' gardens are overflowing with squash and zucchini. One of the classic French favorites is the mix of squash, eggplant, peppers and tomato known as ratatouille. It's a great celebration of the summer harvest, and it's one of those recipes that you can vary depending on what's most bountiful. More squash than eggplant? It really doesn't matter that much. The blend and variety of ingredients is inexact. Ratatouille is substantial enough to be a lunch on its own served with crusty bread, served over couscous or pasta, or as an accompaniment to grilled fish or meat. So when your neighbors arrive bearing armfuls of squash, you know what to make.

1. Cut the vegetables into fairly large chunks. If they are cut too small they tend to fall apart when braised.

2. In a large heavy bottomed pot, lightly brown the onions in a little olive oil. When brown, add the squash, zucchini, eggplant, and peppers, and lightly toss as they are browned over moderate heat, for about 2-3 minutes.

3. Add the herbs and garlic, and then add the tomatoes, and let simmer for about 15 minutes.

4. The vegetables need to be soft, but shouldn't be mushy. Serve alone or as an accompaniment.

1 Spanish onion, peeled and sliced

olive oil

1 yellow summer squash, diced

1 zucchini, diced

1 eggplant, diced

1 red pepper, sliced

1 yellow pepper, sliced

1 tablespoon minced garlic

pinch fresh chopped oregano

pinch fresh chopped rosemary

pinch fresh chopped thyme

½ teaspoon fennel seeds

3 cups peeled, diced tomatoes

salt and pepper

ROASTED PARSNIPS
Serves 4

The key to a great Thanksgiving meal is a variety of interesting side dishes. The turkey and stuffing are obligatory, as are cranberry sauce and sweet potatoes in some form, so most of the menu is prescribed. But there still is some room for creativity, and it's the perfect meal to serve one of the most ignored and forgotten vegetables in America: the parsnip. Parsnips look like white carrots, but their distinctive flavor is even "rootier" than carrots or celery root. Preparing parsnips is simple. Just peel them, cut them in large chunks, toss with a little melted butter and fresh herbs, and roast at 350° for about 30 minutes until pleasantly browned.

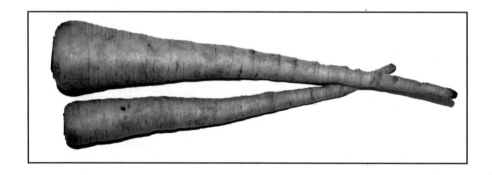

8 large parsnips

3 tablespoons butter

dash salt and pepper

pinch fresh thyme

1. Preheat oven to 350°

2. Peel the parsnips, and cut into large finger-sized chunks.

3. Toss the parsnips with the melted butter, salt and pepper, and herbs.

4. Roast for about 20 minutes, or until well browned.

SLOW ROASTED VEGETABLES

Serves 6-8

When it is too cold outside to use your outdoor grill to prepare grilled vegetables, it is time to consider preparing slow roasted vegetables in the oven indoors. Slow roasting vegetables is a way to sample some of the vegetables that many of us don't eat too often. Parsnips, turnips and celery root are delicious together, and also when mixed with carrots, apples and onions. The precise ration and combination of vegetables may easily be varied to suit your taste, or to what you have available. Whether served as an accompaniment to a roast, or with a grain like couscous or brown rice as an entree, they are simple to make, and last well in the refrigerator for a few days.

1. Preheat oven to 300°

2. After peeling all the vegetables, cut them into a uniform ½" dice, and combine together in a mixing bowl.

3. Toss the vegetables with the melted butter, salt and pepper, and minced fresh thyme.

4. Lay out on a flat baking sheet, and bake for 45 minutes to an hour. Stir the vegetables every once in a while to prevent sticking and burning. Check for doneness after about 40 minutes. When the vegetables are soft, they are done.

5. Serve hot with any roasted or grilled meat, or simply spread on hot baguette.

2 large carrots, peeled

1 medium sized celery root, peeled

2 parsnips, peeled

1 turnip, peeled

2 Granny Smith apples, peeled

1 cup small shallots or pearl onions

3 tablespoons melted butter

salt and pepper

fresh thyme

OVEN-ROASTED TOMATOES
Serves 4

For most of the year we just dream about being able to eat real fresh garden tomatoes, and then when the season finally arrives, it's over in a flash. For a few weeks in August there is an abundance of garden tomatoes, and then after Labor Day the season ends. The following recipe for oven-roasted tomatoes is a way to extend the season. These tomatoes are roasted at a very low temperature, the lowest setting on your oven, for about 8-10 hours, and the result is a partially dried tomato that still has quite a bit more moisture than commercially bought sun-dried tomatoes. They can be stored in olive oil in the refrigerator for at least a week or two. A convection oven works best. By the end of summer, nights are cool, and putting these tomatoes in the oven at night before bed is a good way to avoid your kitchen overheating during the day. These tomatoes can be eaten in a sandwich, as part of a salad or antipasto, or sautéed in your favorite fish or chicken dish. Be sure to save and use the olive oil the tomatoes have been roasted in, which has a wonderful tomato-infused flavor.

6 tomatoes

2 cloves garlic, thinly sliced

sprig fresh thyme

⅓ teaspoon coarsely crushed black peppercorns.

1 cup olive oil

1. Preheat the oven to its lowest setting, ideally somewhere between 150°-175°

2. Remove the core of the tomatoes, and cut them in half. Remove the seeds from the center.

3. Place the tomatoes cut side down in a glass or stainless steel pan, and add the remaining ingredients.

4. Bake the tomatoes for about 8 hours.

5. The tomatoes can be eaten when done, or refrigerated for up to two weeks in the olive oil in which they were cooked.

GRILLED CORN ON THE COB

Serves 4

Many people assume that corn on the cob means boiled; the Native Americans were more accustomed to grilling it. There are a variety of schools of corn grilling; some prefer to peel the corn and put it directly on the grill, while others soak the unhusked ear in salt water for awhile, and then grill. Either method works, but I prefer the direct grill method, both because it imparts a more charred flavor, and because peeling the hot grilled corn can be rough on the fingers. The key with corn is always freshness.

1. Peel the husk off the corn, and be sure to remove the fine silk.

2. Be sure the surface of the grill is clean. Use a stiff wire brush to remove particles from the grill. Wipe the surface of the grill with a cloth dipped in a little vegetable oil.

8 ears corn

vegetable oil

salt and pepper

⅓ stick unsalted butter

3. Place the corn directly on the grill, and grill on each side for 2 minutes.

4. Rub with softened butter, salt and pepper, and eat immediately.

GRILLED ASPARAGUS
Serves 4

We often think of asparagus as a delicate vegetable, and it is often treated that way, poached, blanched, or steamed, and served frequently with fish of chicken. But as we begin to dust off the grill for the summer season, remember that one of the items that grills very well is asparagus. Just trim the thick stems off the spears, toss with a little oil in a bowl, and grill for a few minutes, occasionally rotating the spears. A shaving of fresh grated Parmesan, and a drizzle of your best olive oil and balsamic vinegar demonstrate that the best things in life are often the simplest.

1 pound asparagus

drizzle olive oil

drizzle balsamic vinegar

½ cup shaved fresh Parmesan

1. Trim the stems off the asparagus, and toss with a little oil in a shallow mixing bowl.

2. Place the spears on a hot grill, perpendicular to the grates, so they don't fall through the spaces.

3. Grill for about 2 minutes on each side, rotating occasionally.

4. Use a tong to remove the spears from the grill, and place on a plate.

5. Sprinkle the shaved Parmesan cheese over the top, and drizzle with some oil and vinegar. Serve with prosciutto, or just with good bread.

CHILLED ASPARAGUS WITH SESAME SAUCE

Serves 4

The following recipe for chilled asparagus with sesame sauce is a light and colorful way to begin a meal. The sesame sauce is an Asian variation on a homemade mayonnaise, using highly seasoned sesame oil in the dressing. The sauce is made in advance and because the asparagus is served at room temperature, it makes an ideal dish for entertaining large numbers.

2 pounds asparagus

1. Trim the ends off the asparagus. Blanch the trimmed asparagus spears in salted boiling water for about 30 seconds, and then drain and plunge into ice water. When cool, drain well.

Dressing:

1 egg yolk

2. In a small mixing bowl, combine the yolk with the mustard, and whisk in half of the vinegar. Very slowly and gradually add the 2 oils in a slow stream, carefully whisking the sauce before the addition of more oil. Alternate the addition of the oil with the remaining vinegar.

1 teaspoon whole grain mustard

¼ cup rice wine vinegar

1 cup soybean oil

¼ cup dark roasted sesame oil

3. Add the soy sauce and honey, and whisk well.

¼ cup soy sauce

1 tablespoon honey

4. Use a small ladle to pour some sauce onto 4 plates, making sure to completely coat the bottom of the plates. Arrange 6-8 of the asparagus spears on each plate over the sauce. Garnish with toasted sesame seeds.

2 tablespoons toasted sesame seeds

53

SPINACH AND ASPARAGUS TIMBALE
Serves 6

Timbales are round or oval-shaped molds that are used to make a variety of vegetable purée accompaniments. They are somewhere between a vegetable soufflé and a quiche, and make an unusual and colorful vegetable side dish that can be served with either fish or meat. Unlike a soufflé, which depends on beaten egg whites, timbales combine a vegetable purée with eggs and cream to make a rich vegetable pudding. They are baked in small molds that sit in a pan surrounded by water, and cooked at low temperatures.

1. Preheat oven to 300°

2. Remove the stems from the spinach, and place the cleaned, washed leaves in a saucepot with ¼ cup of water, and steam for about 2 minutes in the covered pot.

3. Remove the spinach from the pot, rinse in cold water, and drain the excess water.

4. Purée the spinach in a blender with the eggs.

5. Combine the spinach and egg purée with the heavy cream, dill, diced asparagus, and salt and pepper, and mix well.

6. Lightly grease the timbale molds (ceramic ramekins may be used), and fill them with the vegetable mix.

7. Place the timbales in a water bath. Bake for about 40 minutes. Remove from the oven, unmold, and serve with fish or meat.

1 pound spinach

6 eggs

1 cup heavy cream

½ cup diced asparagus

1 bunch chopped fresh dill

butter or oil

salt and pepper

CELERY ROOT GRATIN
Serves 4

Scalloped potatoes are an old traditional favorite, but substituting celery root for the potatoes yields a similar dish with a more interesting flavor. Take care to remove all the gnarly skin from the surface of the celery root, and then slice just like a potato. The rest of the procedure is almost exactly the same. This makes a great winter accompaniment to roasts and game dishes.

1. Preheat oven to 350°

2. Cook the onion in a little oil slowly for about 15 minutes until it is golden brown.

3. Combine the sliced celery root with the sautéed onion and remaining ingredients in a large bowl, and mix well.

4. Pour the mix into a small baking dish, and cover with aluminum foil.

5. Bake covered for about 45 minutes, and then remove the foil and bake an additional 15 minutes. Serve warm.

1 onion, peeled and thinly sliced

olive oil

3 large celery root, peeled and thinly sliced

4 eggs

1 cup heavy cream

pinch salt and pepper

½ cup grated cheese(Swiss or Parmesan)

1 tablespoon caraway seeds

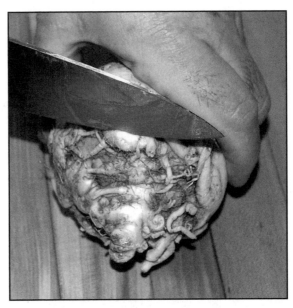

PASTA

Angel Hair with
Asparagus and Shaved Parmesan • 60

Linguini with Shrimp
in Spicy Tomato Sauce • 61

Fettuccine with Berkshire
Blue Cheese • 62

Spinach and Ricotta Gnocchi • 63

Orzo with Shrimp and Saffron • 64

Fettuccine Bolognese • 65

Saffron Risotto Cakes • 66

Cellophane Noodles with
Sesame Sauce • 67

Fettuccine with Asparagus and
Shiitake Mushrooms • 68

Three Little Pig Pasta • 69

ANGEL HAIR WITH ASPARAGUS
AND SHAVED PARMESAN
Serves 6

There are few cooking items with as much variation in quality as Parmesan cheese. Real Parmesan cheese comes in giant wheels and is one of the most long-aged cheeses there is. It is sold in chunks to be ground freshly for later use. What is sold in canisters and bags already ground has so little flavor as to bear almost no resemblance to the real thing. You can use a vegetable peeler on a chunk of fresh Parmesan to shave off thin slices of the cheese, which make a garnish on pasta. Mounded on top of some angel hair pasta tossed with asparagus and garlic butter, it makes for a great meal.

1 bunch asparagus,
cut in small pieces

1 red pepper, in
julienne slices

½ teaspoon
minced garlic

olive oil

½ cup white wine

⅔ stick unsalted
butter

1 pound angel hair
pasta, cooked

1 cup Parmesan
cheese shavings

1. In a skillet, sauté the asparagus and red pepper in a little oil, then add the garlic.

2. Add the white wine, let reduce, and whisk in the butter a little at a time.

3. Toss the asparagus with the warm pasta, and mix well. Ladle the pasta into serving bowls, and garnish the top with the shaved Parmesan cheese. Serve immediately.

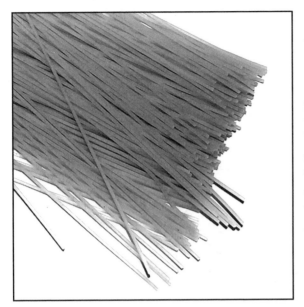

LINGUINI WITH SHRIMP IN SPICY TOMATO SAUCE
Serves 4

Considering how quick and easy it is to prepare home-made tomato sauce for pasta, there's little reason to buy the commercially prepared jarred version in the supermarket. A generous quantity of garlic, balsamic vinegar and a sprinkling of crushed red pepper flakes can transform some canned tomatoes in just a short while. A few shrimp or scallops can complete the dish, and constitute a substantial entrée.

1. Heat a little olive oil in a heavy bottomed sauce pot, add the onions, and when golden, add the garlic, crushed red pepper flakes, bay leaf and vinegar. Add the tomatoes.

2. Let the sauce simmer for 15 minutes

3. Add some olive oil to a large skillet, and sauté the shrimp for about 2 minutes on each side.

4. Toss the cooked linguini with the sauce in a large mixing bowl, and divide among 4 plates. Top with the sautéed shrimp, and serve immediately.

2 twelve-ounce cans of peeled, diced plum tomatoes

1 Spanish onion, peeled and diced

olive oil

1 tablespoon minced garlic

1 bay leaf

1 teaspoon crushed red pepper flakes

¼ cup balsamic vinegar

16 large shrimp

1 pound linguini, cooked

FETTUCCINE WITH BERKSHIRE BLUE CHEESE

Serves 4

The cover story of an issue of *Wine Spectator Magazine* featured an article on the world's best cheeses, and included among them was Berkshire Blue cheese from High Lawn Farm. While many blue cheeses tend to be dry and crumbly, like some varieties of Stilton and Gorgonzola, Berkshire Blue is rich and creamy. It makes a delicious sauce for pasta. Walnuts are a traditional accompaniment to blue cheese, and provide the garnish for this dish. Of course, other blue cheeses may be substituted.

1 pound fettuccine

1 teaspoon minced shallots

1 tablespoon butter

1 teaspoon minced fresh thyme

2 tablespoons flour

1 cup chicken stock

1 cup heavy cream

¾ pound Berkshire Blue cheese

2 tablespoons roasted chopped walnuts

1. Cook the fettuccine, and reserve for later.

2. In a saucepot, heat the butter, add the shallots, and stir well. When lightly browned, add thyme and the flour, and stir well.

3. Add the chicken stock and cream, and mix well to incorporate the flour. Stir well as the sauce thickens.

4. Lower the heat to a low simmer, and whisk in the cheese, stirring well.

5. To serve, reheat the noodles and toss with the sauce. Garnish with the toasted walnuts.

SPINACH AND RICOTTA GNOCCHI
Serves 4

Gnocchi are an Italian dumpling usually made out of potato. The following recipe is for a slightly different kind of gnocchi, which includes a purée of spinach and ricotta, and properly made, they are light as a feather. They are sometimes served in broth, or with pesto, or even with a traditional red sauce. They are not difficult to make, but the ones made at home are almost always better than those in restaurants.

1. Steam the cleaned, stemmed spinach with just 2 tablespoons of water in a heavy-bottomed, covered saucepot. Let cool. Purée in a food processor or blender.

2. Combine the cheeses, egg, spinach purée, flour and seasonings in a bowl, and mix well. Allow to chill for at least an hour.

3. When dough is chilled, form small golf ball sized balls out of the dough, and drop into vigorously boiling salted water for about 3-4 minutes. They are done when they rise to the surface.

4. Remove them from the water with a slotted spoon.

5. The gnocchi may be served in chicken broth; gratinéed with Parmesan cheese on top; with a red sauce, or with pesto.

8 ounces cleaned, stemmed spinach

1 cup grated Parmesan cheese

1 egg, beaten

1 cup ricotta cheese

½ cup flour

salt and pepper

fresh thyme

ORZO WITH SHRIMP AND SAFFRON

Orzo is pasta made into the shape of rice. The tiny beads expand and cook more like rice than like pasta, but the soft chewy consistency is like pasta. Orzo is frequently used in soup, as sort of a variation on barley. The orzo and the shrimp must be cooked separately, then blended together. This is delicious either hot or cold.

1 pound orzo

vegetable oil

½ pound peeled and deveined shrimp

pinch saffron

1 tablespoon minced garlic

½ cup white wine

1 cup frozen peas

¼ cup grated Parmesan cheese

3 tablespoons melted butter

salt and pepper

1. Cook the orzo in a large quantity of salted water like you would any pasta, and then drain well. Cool, and toss with a little vegetable oil to prevent from sticking together.

2. In a large skillet, sauté the shrimp with the garlic and saffron for about 2 minutes, add the wine, and let reduce.

3. In large pot, combine the cooked orzo and cooked shrimp, and add the peas. Add the melted butter, and stir well. Season with salt and pepper. When warm, add the cheese, and stir well. Serve immediately.

FETTUCCINE BOLOGNESE
Serves 4

One of the differences between standard commercially raised beef and pasture-raised grass-fed beef is that the meat is much leaner. Those who have browned ground beef in a skillet to make a traditional meat sauce know how much fat is rendered in the process, which must be drained and discarded. Grass-fed beef is much leaner, and while that makes it somewhat more problematic for use in hamburgers, it is an ideal quality when making a Bolognese sauce. If you have access to grass-fed beef, you will surely notice the difference it makes in this recipe.

1 pound ground beef

1 Spanish onion, peeled and sliced

olive oil

1 bay leaf

1 tablespoon minced garlic

1 quart peeled, diced tomatoes

1 cup grated Parmesan cheese

salt and pepper

1 pound cooked fettuccine

1. Brown the meat in a skillet, drain and discard the fat, and reserve the beef.

2. In a heavy bottom saucepot, brown the onions in a little olive oil and then add the bay leaf and garlic. Let cook 1 minute. Add the tomatoes, beef, and salt and pepper.

3. Let simmer for 30 minutes, and then stir in the cheese. Toss with fettuccine and serve hot.

65

SAFFRON RISOTTO CAKES
Serves 4

The most common way to eat risotto is as a creamy hot rice dish, which has the consistency of oatmeal. Served with seafood, mushrooms or vegetables, it is a classic of northern Italian cuisine. Leftover risotto can be formed into little cakes and fried. They will be rich and creamy. When risotto is cooked and then chilled, it is easy to form and mold into cakes. The fried cakes make a delicious appetizer, or accompaniment to sautéed shrimp or scallops.

1 cup arborio rice

butter or olive oil

1 teaspoon minced shallots

pinch saffron

3-4 cups chicken stock

¼ cup Parmesan cheese

1. Preheat oven to 350°

2. Sauté the rice and shallots in a little butter or olive oil, and the saffron. Stir well, and slowly add a little of the chicken stock.

3. Allow the rice to slowly absorb the liquid, and gradually add more stock as it is absorbed into the rice. It will take about 25 minutes for the rice to cook, with several gradual additions of the stock.

4. When the rice is tender, add the cheese, and mix well.

5. Remove the cooked risotto from the pot, and pour onto a flat baking sheet. Use a spoon to spread the cooked risotto to an even thickness. Allow the rice to cool for several hours or overnight.

6. To make the cakes, form the rice into hockey puck-sized discs.

7. Fry the cakes for about 2 minutes on each side until lightly browned, and then bake for about 3 minutes. Serve with sautéed shrimp or scallops.

CELLOPHANE NOODLES WITH SESAME SAUCE
Serves 4-6

Cellophane noodles are thin Asian noodles made from mung beans, which are almost translucent in color, and slightly chewy. They can be eaten chilled or hot, and are the basis of a wide variety of Asian noodle dishes. The following recipe is easy to prepare, and delicious eaten chilled.

1. Cook the noodles in salted water for about 4 minutes, or until soft. Cool and drain well.

2. Sauté the shiitake mushrooms. Set aside.

3. To make the dressing, place the peanut butter in a mixer or bowl, add the remaining ingredients and mix well until smooth.

4. To assemble, combine the noodles with the sauce and vegetables, including mushrooms, in a large mixing bowl, and toss well. Serve chilled.

1 pound cellophane noodles

1 cup shiitake mushrooms, thinly sliced

Dressing:

1 cup peanut butter

¼ cup sesame oil

½ cup soy sauce

1 teaspoon minced ginger

1 teaspoon minced garlic

4 tablespoons honey

2 tablespoons rice wine vinegar

1 julienne carrot

1 julienne red pepper

1 seedless cucumber, thinly sliced

½ pound mung bean sprouts

FETTUCCINE WITH ASPARAGUS AND SHIITAKE MUSHROOMS

Serves 4

The arrival of daylight saving's time comes just about the same time that local asparagus begins appearing in the markets, and together they herald the arrival of a time of year when lighter foods seem more appealing. A simple sauté of some tender asparagus spears with a few mushrooms, tossed with some pasta, is all you need to create a delicious meal. A splash of soy sauce and sherry provide the accent.

olive oil

1 teaspoon minced shallots

½ pound shiitake mushrooms

1 pound asparagus spears, stems removed, diced

½ teaspoon minced garlic

splash soy sauce

splash sherry

1 pound fettuccine, cooked al dente

1. Heat a little olive oil in a skillet, and lightly brown the shallots.

2. Add the mushrooms, asparagus and garlic, and toss well.

3. Add the soy sauce and sherry, toss the vegetable mix with the cooked pasta, and serve immediately.

The combination of prosciutto, smoked bacon and sausage makes for a delicious and rich base for pasta. And of course, given these ingredients, the pasta shape that is most appropriate is that of the spiral, which resembles a pig's twisted tail. Instead of using the presliced strips of bacon, a chunk of heavily smoked slab bacon has much more flavor. And while a traditional cream sauce is made almost entirely of cream, by using chicken stock for half of the liquid the sauce will not be quite so rich.

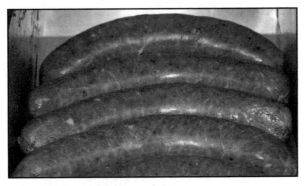

4 links pork sausage

¼ pound prosciutto, finely chopped

¼ pound smoked bacon, cut in cubes

1 Spanish onion, peeled and sliced

pinch fresh thyme and basil

½ teaspoon minced garlic

2 cups chicken stock

2 cups heavy cream

½ cup grated Parmesan cheese

1 bunch scallion, minced

1 pound corkscrew pasta, cooked

1. Preheat oven to 350°

2. Place the sausage links on a baking pan and bake for 25 minutes, turning them over once. When cooked, drain and discard any rendered fat, pat dry with paper towels, and dice the sausage into small pieces.

3. Cook the bacon until crisp, and drain off any excess fat.

4. In a small saucepot, sauté the onion until well browned, and add the garlic and herbs. Add cream and let reduce by ⅓. Add the chicken stock and let simmer on low heat for about 30 minutes. Then whisk in the grated cheese and stir in the prosciutto and cooked bacon and sausage. Toss with the cooked pasta, garnish with the scallion, and serve immediately.

SEAFOOD

Saffron Shellfish Sampler • 72

Calamari in Garlic Sauce • 73

Sautéed Red Snapper Niçoise • 74

Grilled Swordfish with Black
Olive and Tomato Salsa • 75

Almond Crusted Brook Trout
With Ginger Orange Sauce • 76

Walnut Crusted Salmon with Arugula,
Orange and Shaved Fennel • 77

Shad Roe with Bacon and Onions • 78

Brook Trout Stuffed
with Mushrooms • 80

Fried Shrimp Dumplings • 83

Halibut with Fresh Tarragon,
Mushroom, and Tomato • 84

Sea Scallops with
Turnip Greens • 85

Striped Bass with Shaved
Fennel and Pernod • 86

Striped Bass with Wilted Spinach • 87

Sautéed Salmon with Asparagus and
Saffron Sauce • 88

Cedar Planked Salmon with
Dijon Maple Glaze • 89

Pan Seared Salmon with
Autumn Vegetables • 90

Salmon with Braised Beets • 92

Roasted Salmon with
Roasted Root Vegetables • 94

Sautéed Shrimp with
Angel Hair Pasta, Garlic Sauce • 95

Vegetable Crusted Filet of Sole • 96

Sea Scallops with McCoun
Apples and Coconut Milk • 97

Sea Scallops in Lemongrass Broth • 98

SAFFRON SHELLFISH SAMPLER

Serves 4

Broth:

1 onion, thinly sliced

olive oil

2 quarts peeled, diced tomatoes

1 bulb fennel, thinly sliced

1 red pepper, thinly sliced

1 bay leaf

3 cups dry white wine

2 teaspoons minced garlic

pinch saffron

½ teaspoon crushed red pepper flakes (optional)

1 pound mussels, cleaned and washed

16 large shrimp, peeled and deveined

1 pound sea scallops

1 dozen steamer clams

One of the classic seafood dishes from Spain and Portugal is a blend of shellfish served in a saffron tomato broth. The idea is similar to a bouillabaisse from the south of France, but the Iberian version is exclusively shellfish, without a flatfish like snapper or bass. The broth is made from a strongly seasoned combination of white wine, tomato, garlic and saffron, and can include any combination of shrimp, scallops, mussels and clams. The broth can be made ahead of time. To serve, just cook the shellfish in the liquid. As the shells open up, they release the slightly salty ocean water into the broth, which imparts extra flavor.

1. In a heavy bottomed saucepot, lightly brown the onion in some olive oil, and then add all the remaining broth ingredients.

2. Cover the pot, and let simmer on low to moderate heat for about 30 minutes.

3. The broth can be prepared ahead of time. When ready to serve, add the shellfish directly into the pot, let simmer about 10 minutes, and then ladle into bowls and serve with crusty garlic bread.

CALAMARI IN GARLIC SAUCE

Serves 4

The trick when preparing calamari is not to overcook it, which is quite easy to do. With just an extra minute of cooking, rings of squid can transform from being tender into inedible rubber bands. The following recipe is easy to prepare, and delicious to eat with some bread to soak up the sauce. Save yourself some of the aggravation by buying squid that has already been cleaned.

1. Using a large knife, slice the squid body into rings, as thinly as possible. Cut the tentacles into smaller pieces, making them easier to eat.

2. In a skillet, combine the garlic, white wine and butter with the red pepper flakes, cover, and simmer for about 2 minutes until reduced and thickened.

3. Add the squid, and cook for 1 minute only.

4. Remove the top, and divide the calamari among 4 plates. Garnish with the parsley and red pepper dice. Serve immediately, with good bread.

2 pounds cleaned squid

½ teaspoon minced garlic

1 tablespoon butter

½ cup white wine

dash crushed red pepper flakes

1 teaspoon minced parsley

1 tablespoon diced red peppers

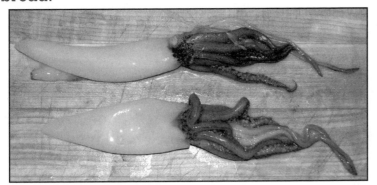

SAUTÉED RED SNAPPER NIÇOISE

Serves 4

The prospect of sautéing fish scares some novice cooks, but it's really a simple and fast way to prepare fish. It requires a little more skill than simply baking fish in the oven, but the results are worth the effort. By adding some vegetables into the skillet along with the fish, in this case red snapper, the result is a complete meal in a pan. The classic Niçoise ingredients are garlic, black olives, and tomatoes, which with the addition of some zucchini and white wine, complete the dish.

4 red snapper filets, 6-8 ounces each

flour

2 pinches minced fresh thyme

olive oil

½ zucchini, diced

1 teaspoon minced shallots

½ teaspoon minced garlic

½ cup peeled and seeded tomatoes, diced

2 tablespoons black olives, pitted

½ teaspoon capers

½ cup white wine

salt and pepper

1. Preheat oven to 350°

2. Dredge the snapper filets in a little flour, and season with salt, pepper and thyme.

3. Heat a little olive oil in a skillet and add the fish filets. Brown for 2 minutes, and then flip over with a spatula.

4. Add the shallots, zucchini, remaining fresh thyme, and garlic into the pan, and sauté for 2 minutes.

5. Add the tomato, capers, olives, and wine, and place the skillet in the oven for 3 minutes.

6. Remove from the oven, remove the fish from the pan and place on 4 plates. Spoon the sauce and vegetables over the top. Serve immediately.

GRILLED SWORDFISH WITH BLACK OLIVE AND TOMATO SALSA
Serves 4

A pinkish tinge of the flesh of fish is an indicator of quality. A quickly prepared salad of sun-dried tomatoes with black olives makes a perfect accompaniment to grilled fish.

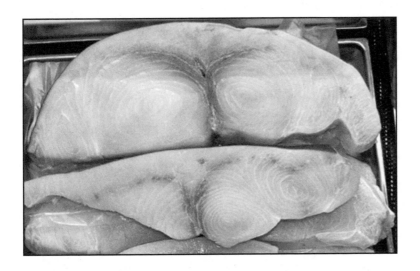

4 swordfish filets, 6-8 ounces each

Salsa:

1 cup sun-dried tomatoes

1 cup black olives, diced

1 bunch scallion, minced

1 teaspoon capers

1 clove garlic, minced

1 tablespoon minced basil leaves

3 tablespoons extra virgin olive oil

1 tablespoon red wine vinegar

1. Soak the dried tomatoes in hot water for at least 30 minutes, than drain and rinse several times to remove excess salt. Slice the dried tomatoes in thin slices.

2. Chop the black olives, and combine them together with the remaining ingredients and mix well.

3. Grill the swordfish for about 2 minutes on each side. Be careful not to overcook the fish.

4. Serve the fish with a dollop of the tomato and olive salsa.

ALMOND CRUSTED BROOK TROUT
WITH GINGER ORANGE SAUCE

Serves 4

While trout almandine may seem like a tired culinary warhorse, the version below yields a crisp and substantial dish, which can be easily prepared and cooks quickly. The technique involves coating the fish in the familiar flour and eggs, with the final application of lightly ground almonds. The sauce can be made directly in the pan.

4 boneless brook trout, heads removed

2 cups flour

3 eggs, beaten

vegetable oil

1½ cups lightly ground blanched sliced almonds

1 cup fresh squeezed orange juice

grated zest of 1 orange

1 tablespoon minced fresh ginger

1. Preheat oven to 350°

2. Place the flour, beaten eggs, and lightly ground almonds in 3 separate bowls.

3. Dip the trout filet flesh side (as opposed to the skin side) first in the flour, then the beaten egg, and finally in the ground almonds, so that the filet is well covered with the nuts.

4. Heat some vegetable oil in a large skillet and place the trout first with the nut side down in the skillet, and cook for 1 minute. Then flip the fish over on the other side and cook for another minute.

5. Place the skillet in the oven for 4 minutes

6. Remove the skillet from the oven, and take out the trout.

7. Add the orange juice and zest and minced ginger to the skillet, and let reduce by half.

8. Pour the sauce over the cooked fish, and serve immediately.

WALNUT CRUSTED SALMON
WITH ARUGULA, ORANGE & SHAVED FENNEL
Serves 4

The key to this dish is vibrant fresh arugula, which tends to wilt quickly. The combination of walnut, orange and fennel is delicious. It helps to shave the raw fennel as thinly as possible. The dressing is made from walnut oil, which has a pronounced flavor, and some orange juice is substituted for the vinegar in the dressing, making it less acidic.

1. Preheat oven to 350°

2. Press the salmon filets into the chopped walnuts, and then place the filets, nut side up, on a baking dish, and bake for about 5 minutes.

3. For the dressing, grate the zest of the orange, and save the rest of the orange. Combine the zest in a bowl with the egg yolk, rice vinegar and mustard, and slowly whisk in the walnut oil, a little bit a time, whisking well before each addition of oil. Add the orange juice last.

4. Use a paring knife to trim away the entire outside skin of the orange. Slice between the orange sections, separate them, and reserve.

5. In a large mixing bowl, toss the shaved fennel and arugula with the dressing, and place the mixture on 4 plates.

6. Remove the salmon from the oven, and place on top of the dressed arugula, in the center of the plate.

7. Place the orange sections around the fish, drizzle a little additional dressing over the top, and serve immediately.

4 six-ounce salmon filets

½ cup finely chopped walnuts

1 orange

1 egg yolk

⅙ cup rice wine vinegar

1 teaspoon Dijon mustard

1 cup walnut oil

⅙ cup freshly squeezed orange juice

1 head fennel. very finely sliced

1 pound arugula

SHAD ROE WITH BACON & ONIONS
Serves 4

Like the swallows to San Capistrano, the return of the shad to the rivers of New England is one of the surest signs of spring. When their sac of roe is full and they are ready to spawn, the shad return to the fresh waters of New England to the awaiting nets of local fisherman. The Hudson and Connecticut rivers are two of the most important area rivers for shad. Because the flesh of the filets are unusually bony and difficult to remove, shad are perhaps more known for their roe than flesh. Sometimes called the "poor man's caviar," the sacs of roe contain thousands of tiny eggs that resemble caviar. One legacy of the Portuguese fishermen who settled parts of eastern New England is the tradition of preparing seafood with either bacon or sausage, as in the following recipe for shad roe with bacon and onions.

1 Spanish onion, peeled and sliced

vegetable oil

2 pair shad roe

1 cup fish or chicken stock

2 teaspoons rice vinegar

8 strips cooked bacon

1. Preheat oven to 350°

2. Sauté the onion slowly in a skillet until it's golden brown, and set aside.

3. Separate the membrane that connects the 2 sacs of roe, and carefully wash the roe to remove any blood or attached fish scales.

4. In a large skillet, sauté the roe in a little oil for about 2 minutes, and then carefully turn over the roe and sauté on the other side. Handle the roe as carefully as possible to avoid tearing open the delicate sacs.

5. To complete cooking the roe, place the entire skillet inside the oven for about 5 minutes.

6. Return the skillet to the stove top, add the onions, vinegar and stock to the skillet, and let the sauce simmer until the volume of liquid has reduced by ⅔.

7. To serve, place one sac of roe on each of 4 plates, pour some of the sauce over them, and top with some of the crisp bacon. Serve immediately.

BROOK TROUT STUFFED WITH MUSHROOMS
Serves 4

Boneless brook trout are available in good fish markets throughout the year, and they can be easily stuffed to make a filling entrée. They're usually sold with the head on, but those who are squeamish can have the head removed. By stuffing the cavity with a filling, the fish can be baked so it's standing up like an "A," which makes for a great presentation. A variety of different stuffings are possible, but the following one for a mushroom stuffing is easy and delicious.

4 brook trout, 8-10 ounces each

1 medium onion, peeled and sliced

olive oil

1 pound mushrooms

1 bunch scallion, minced

pinch fresh thyme

splash sherry

white wine

1. Preheat oven to 375°

2. Wash the trout under water, and pat dry.

3. In a skillet, lightly brown the onion in a little olive oil, add the mushrooms, scallions and thyme and cook until soft. Deglaze with the sherry.

4. Place the mushroom mix in a colander and allow to drain for about 15 minutes.

5. Purée the mix in a food processor, using the pulse button. Leave the mixture slightly coarse, and be careful not to overprocess.

6. Take the mushroom mix and fill the cavity of the trout. Stand the stuffed trout up on a baking dish. Splash with a little white wine and bake for about 10 minutes. Serve immediately.

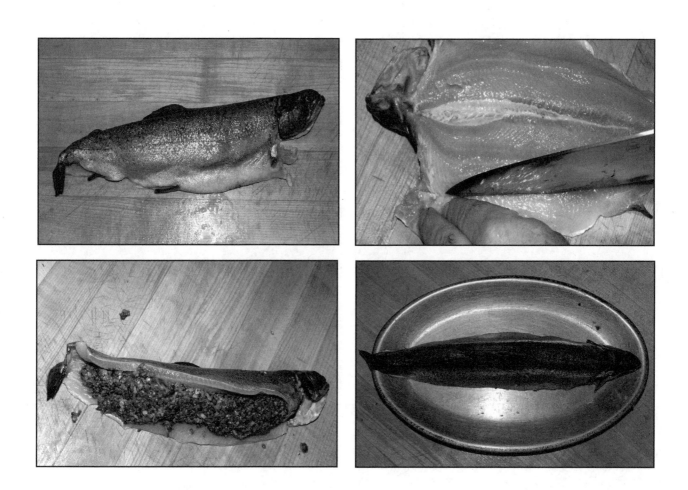

FRIED SHRIMP DUMPLINGS

Serves 6-8

Ingredients that were once rare and hard to find are now commonly available in gourmet markets. One of those ingredients is Chinese dumpling dough, which is used to make wontons. These can easily be made at home. The dumplings can be filled with a variety of different ingredients. The following recipe is easy to make. Though they can be steamed or boiled, I think they taste better fried.

1. Cook the shrimp in a skillet with the curry powder. Allow to drain, and cool.

2. Purée the cooked shrimp in a food processor.

3. Mix the shrimp with the minced scallion.

4. Lay the dumpling dough out on a counter. Use a pastry brush to brush the edges of the dough with the egg wash, which will help seal the dumpling.

5. Fill the dumpling with about a tablespoon of filling, and then press together the sides of the dough to seal the filling, making a half-moon shape.

6. Toss the dumplings in the cornstarch so that they are thoroughly covered.

7. Fill a large pot with about 1 quart of oil and fry the dumplings in hot oil for about 2 minutes. If you prefer, they can also be boiled. Serve with soy sauce.

1 pound mini shrimp

1 tablespoon curry powder

1 bunch scallion, minced

1 package dumpling dough

1 egg, beaten

frying oil

2 cups cornstarch

soy sauce

HALIBUT WITH FRESH TARRAGON, MUSHROOM, AND TOMATO

Serves 4

Fresh halibut is in season in the summer, and lower in price than at other times of the year. Halibut from the West Coast and Alaska is plentiful in the market. Halibut is sort of like jumbo sole, and the white flesh is meaty and moist. Before serving, remove the dark skin, which can be tough to chew. The technique of sautéing fish with mushrooms and tomato is known as "bon femme" in French, and just plain old delicious in English.

butter or olive oil

4 halibut filets,
6-8 ounces each

1 tablespoon
minced shallots

½ pound mushrooms, sliced

1 cup diced fresh or
roasted tomatoes

1 bunch tarragon, chopped

1 cup white wine

1. Heat some butter or olive oil in a large skillet, and add the halibut. Brown on one side for about 2 minutes, and then flip over the filets with a spatula.

2. Add the shallots, mushrooms, tarragon and chopped tomato in the skillet, and allow to cook 2 more minutes.

3. Add the wine, place a lid over the skillet and allow the fish to cook for another 2 minutes.

4. Remove the lid, check the fish for doneness (the fish should flake apart easily when a fork is inserted), and then let some of the liquid reduce. Serve immediately.

SEA SCALLOPS WITH TURNIP GREENS

Serves 4

Most of us north of the Mason Dixon Line are not accustomed to eating turnip greens, but that is not true in the Deep South. When the turnips are growing and the roots are still small, the green leafy tops make for delicious eating. The taste is a little sharper than many of us are used to, and they require cooking or braising to soften the flavors. They are traditionally served with pork or cooked in pork fat, but the fat conscious among us may want to modify or update this usage. The following recipe for sea scallops with turnip greens was probably never served at Tara, but is nonetheless a delicious modern adaptation of one of the Deep South's favorites.

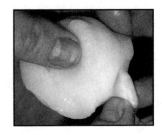

1. Clean the scallops well, and be sure to remove the little tough side muscle from them.

2. Wash the turnip greens well. Chop coarsely, leaving in large pieces.

3. In a large skillet, heat a little oil and add the shallots. Stir well until lightly browned.

4. Add the scallops and sauté for 2 minutes, stirring well. Then add the garlic, turnip greens and tomatoes, tossing vigorously. The greens should be slightly wilted but not completely overcooked and soggy. Add the splash of vinegar.

5. Whisk in the butter, if using, remove from the pan immediately and divide among 4 plates. Serve with rice.

2 pounds sea scallops

2 bunches turnip greens (about ½ pound)

vegetable oil

1 teaspoon minced shallots

½ teaspoon minced garlic

½ cup peeled, seeded, diced tomatoes

balsamic vinegar

1 tablespoon butter, (optional)

2 cups cooked rice

STRIPED BASS WITH
SHAVED FENNEL AND PERNOD
Serves 2-4

One of the classic beverages of any self-respecting French café is Pernod or Ricard. The anise-flavored liqueur is usually drunk straight or mixed with water, but can also be used in cooking. Fennel is an anise-flavored vegetable that looks a little like celery, with a thick bulb at the bottom, long stalks, and fronds at the top that look like dill. Only the bulb is really edible, but save some of the fronds on top as a garnish. Slice the fennel as thinly as possible, so it retains its crispness and crunch in this dish. A little splash of the liqueur is used in the following recipe to reinforce the anise flavor of the fennel, which is delicious with striped bass or other freshwater fish. Striped bass are one of the success stories of environmental protection. Highly endangered a few decades ago, their stocks have been replenished and the season has been extended. Availability of these delicious fish is greater now than in years past.

4 striped bass filets, 6-8 ounces each

flour

olive oil

1 bulb fennel, thinly sliced

1 tomato, peeled and diced

pinch chopped fresh thyme

¼ cup white wine

¼ teaspoon minced fresh garlic

splash Pernod

1 tablespoon butter

1. Preheat oven to 350°

2. Lightly toss the fish in a little flour. Heat a little olive oil in a skillet, and when hot, brown the filets on each side for about 2 minutes.

3. Add the sliced fennel to the pan, add the tomato, thyme, garlic and wine, and place the skillet in the oven for about 4 minutes.

4. Remove the skillet from the oven, add a splash of Pernod, and swirl in a little butter. Place the filets on a plate, mound the fennel and tomato mix on top of the filets and serve immediately.

STRIPED BASS WITH WILTED SPINACH
Serves 4

Amidst the widespread and growing concern about the dangers of eating farm-raised salmon, one bright spot is the recovery of the wild striped bass population. Years ago these fish were subject to very stringent fishing regulations, and since then their numbers have rebounded strongly. Only a short time ago the season was limited to a few short weeks of summer, but now the season has been extended. This is good news for fish lovers. The following recipe for striped bass with spinach is not difficult to prepare, and can be made in under 30 minutes. Be careful not to cook the spinach too long, or it will cook down to almost nothing.

1. Preheat oven to 375°

2. Dredge the fish filets in flour. In a hot skillet with a little butter or oil, lightly brown the fish on all sides.

3. Place the skillet in the oven for about 5 minutes to finish cooking.

4. Remove the skillet from the oven, take the fish out of the pan, and place it on a plate.

5. Return the skillet to the stovetop, add the shallots, and let lightly brown for 1 minute. Add the chopped tomato and spinach and toss quickly, for about 30 seconds. Add the wine, and then swirl in the butter.

6. To serve, drape the cooked spinach over the top of the bass filets, and serve immediately.

4 striped bass filets, 6-8 ounces each

flour

butter or oil

1 teaspoon minced shallot

2 tablespoons chopped fresh tomato

12 ounces cleaned spinach

splash white wine

1 teaspoon butter

SAUTÉED SALMON WITH ASPARAGUS AND SAFFRON SAUCE
Serves 2-4

Few dishes could be more spring-like than salmon and asparagus. When served with a saffron sauce, the pale pastel colors of orange salmon, yellow saffron and green asparagus are the epitome of spring. The whole dish cooks in just minutes on top of the stove. The key is slicing the salmon into thin slices instead of one large, 6-ounce steak or filet. It only takes a pinch of saffron to make the dish.

12 thin slices of salmon filet, about 2 ounces each

vegetable oil

1 tablespoon minced shallots

1 cup asparagus spears, ends removed, diced

¼ cup white wine

pinch saffron

¼ cup heavy cream

1. Heat a little vegetable oil in a skillet and add the salmon pieces and shallots. Sauté for about 1 minute and then turn over the pieces with a spatula.

2. Add the asparagus spears and sauté for another minute.

3. Add the white wine and saffron, and let reduce until almost evaporated. Then add the cream.

4. As the sauce turns the classic saffron color, divide the salmon and asparagus, put on plates and serve with the sauce.

CEDAR PLANKED SALMON WITH DIJON-MAPLE GLAZE

Serves 4

The technique of cooking salmon on cedar planks originated with the Native Americans in the Northwest, but it has become a popular technique across the country. As anyone with a cedar closet knows, cedar is an incredibly aromatic wood, and the wood imparts a distinct flavor to the fish as it cooks. The cedar plank actually catches fire when exposed to an open flame, and the burning smoke adds a definite and delightful smoky flavor to the fish. This must be done with great care, and should not be attempted by novices. A glaze of equal parts maple syrup and Dijon mustard completes the dish.

1. Preheat oven to 400°

2. Soak the cedar in water for at least a half an hour before cooking.

3. Combine the maple syrup and mustard and whisk together. Set aside.

4. Place the salmon on the cedar plank in the oven for about 5 minutes.

5. Remove the cooked salmon on the plank from the oven and carefully expose the plank to an open flame either in a broiler or gas burner flame, and allow the plank to catch fire for just a few seconds. Quickly cover the burning plank with a damp towel to extinguish the flame, allowing the wood to impart flavor to the fish.

6. Drizzle a little sauce over the top of the salmon and serve immediately.

4 pieces of cedar shake

½ cup maple syrup

½ cup Dijon mustard

4 salmon filets, 6-8 ounces each

PAN SEARED SALMON WITH AUTUMN VEGETABLES

Serves 4

If spring is the season for green vegetables, like asparagus and snow peas, then autumn is the season for brown vegetables, like mushrooms, potatoes and onions. The following recipe for sautéed salmon features a mix of autumn vegetables with hues appropriate to the season. For this dish, tiny red and yellow "C" sized potatoes, or potatoes the size of marbles are the best. Small button mushrooms are used whole as well, in keeping with the uniformity of size. The flavor of whole roasted shallots adds to the woodsy quality of the dish. While white wine is appropriate to serve with spring salmon and green vegetables, this dish calls for a soft red wine like pinot noir. With the exception of roasting shallots, this recipe can be made in 10 minutes.

1 cup peeled shallots

butter or oil

½ cup tiny red "C" potatoes

½ cup tiny Yukon "C" potatoes

4 salmon filets, 6-8 ounces each

flour

1 tablespoon butter

1 tablespoon olive oil

pinch fresh tarragon

1 cup button mushrooms

½ cup, peeled, diced, seeded tomatoes

1 tablespoon rice wine vinegar

2 tablespoons soft butter (optional)

1. Preheat oven to 350°

2. Sauté the shallots in a skillet with butter or oil, and then roast in the oven for about 30 minutes until soft and brown. Set aside.

3. Parboil the potatoes in salted water for about 10 minutes until soft, and then drain and set aside. (If you can't find the tiny "C" sized potatoes, you may substitute larger potatoes cut into quarters and blanched.)

4. Dredge the top side of the salmon filet in flour. In a large skillet heat a tablespoon of butter with a tablespoon of oil and brown the floured side of the filet for 2 minutes.

5. Turn the filet over, season with tarragon, and add the mushrooms, potatoes and shallots, and brown for 2 minutes.

6. Place the skillet in the oven for about 7 minutes to complete cooking the salmon. Check for doneness and return the skillet to the stovetop.

7. Add the diced tomato and deglaze with the vinegar, and then slowly whisk in the soft butter, if used.

8. To serve, place the salmon filets in the center of 4 plates, and then surround the fish with the vegetables and sauce. Serve immediately.

SALMON WITH BRAISED BEETS
Serves 4

One of the hallmarks of contemporary cuisine is the substitution of fish for meat in certain traditional or classic dishes, as in tuna tartar, in which tuna replaces the beef. Many people are trying to limit their consumption of red meat, and chefs respond to these trends. While the cold beet soup known as borscht is widely known, there is another beet soup which is served hot in the winter, in which the beets are combined with cabbage, and simmered slowly with a piece of beef, like chuck steak. It is a savory and hearty winter soup. A variation on the same mix makes a delicious way to serve salmon. If you can find beets with the green tops, they make a flavorful and vitamin-packed addition to the mix. A dash of cornstarch helps thicken the mix just enough so that it's not too soupy.

3 beets with tops

¼ head green cabbage

1 Spanish onion, peeled

2 tablespoons sugar

½ teaspoon salt

¼ cup red wine vinegar

1 teaspoon cornstarch

salt and pepper

**4 salmon filets,
6-8 ounces each**

1 bunch chopped dill

3 tablespoons sour cream

1. Wash the beets and tops well. Trim the stems off the bottoms of the beets, and coarsely chop the beet greens.

2. Grate the beets, cabbage and onion in a food processor, or with an old-fashioned, four-sided grater.

3. Place the grated vegetables in a small saucepot, add 3 cups water, the sugar, salt and vinegar. Simmer for 20 minutes.

4. Use a colander to drain off and discard about half the cooking liquid.

5. Return the strained beet mix to the saucepot, dissolve the cornstarch in ¼ cup cold water, add to the beets and simmer for another 2 minutes.

6. Salt and pepper the salmon filets and cook in an oven, grill or broiler for about 7 minutes.

7. Place the beet mix on 4 plates. Place the salmon on top of the beets. Garnish with chopped dill and sour cream.

ROASTED SALMON WITH ROASTED ROOT VEGETABLES
Serves 4

Slowly roasting a blend of root vegetables is an appealing way to serve salmon in the fall. Celery root is an under-utilized autumn root vegetable, with the flavor of celery and the starchiness of potatoes, and is the key to this dish. Combining celery root with equal parts apple, carrot, and onions creates a complex blend of flavors. The apples are sweet and moist, the onions savory, and the carrots and celery root earthy.

1 celery root, peeled and diced

2 carrots, peeled and diced

2 Granny Smith apples, peeled and diced

¾ cup peeled pearl onions

1 teaspoon fresh chopped thyme

3 tablespoons melted butter

salt and pepper

parchment paper

4 salmon filets, 6-8 ounces each

2 tablespoons butter

½ cup white wine

½ cup Chinese hoisin Sauce

2 tablespoons chopped parsley

1. Preheat oven to 275°

2. In a mixing bowl, combine celery root, carrots, apples, pearl onions, and thyme. Add salt and pepper to taste.

3. Pour the melted butter over the vegetables, and toss well.

4. Line a baking pan with parchment paper and roast the vegetables for 45-60 minutes, occasionally stirring and tossing the vegetables. Turn oven up to 400°

5. Place the salmon filets on a baking pan, season with salt and pepper, dot with the butter, and add the wine. Bake for about 5 minutes.

6. Cover 4 plates with the roasted vegetables and place the salmon filets on top. Drizzle with a little of the hoisin sauce, and garnish with the chopped parsley. Serve hot.

94

SAUTÉED SHRIMP
WITH ANGEL HAIR PASTA
Serves 4

Angel hair pasta is the thinnest and most delicate of all pastas, and it must be cooked carefully and handled with care to prevent breaking. It is particularly good with sautéed shrimp and garlic sauce. The fine strands of pasta soak up and absorb the sauce well. Feel free to add any combination of vegetables, including fresh or sun-dried tomatoes, broccoli florets, chopped scallions, or sugar snap peas.

1. Cook the pasta in a large pot of salted water. Drain and cool.

2. In a large skillet, heat a little olive oil and add the shallots and shrimp. Cook the shrimp on one side, then turn over, and add the broccoli, garlic and dried tomatoes.

3. Cook for one more minute, then add the wine. Allow the wine to reduce by half, then swirl in the butter.

4. Toss the sauce and shrimp with the noodles, and serve hot.

1 pound angel hair pasta

24 shrimp, peeled, cleaned, and tails removed

olive oil

1 teaspoon minced shallots

½ cup sun-dried tomatoes

½ teaspoon minced garlic

1 cup broccoli florets

1 cup white wine

4 tablespoons butter

VEGETABLE CRUSTED FILET OF SOLE

Serves 4

The technique of coating or breading fish with breadcrumbs is an old one, which adds a crisp crust to the exterior of the fish while keeping the interior warm and moist. The following recipe is a variation and updating of that idea, which coats the fish in a light and crunchy, brightly colored vegetable layer. Feel free to use a wide variety of brightly colored vegetables in the mix. Because the fish cooks so quickly, the vegetables retain their color.

¼ cup diced red pepper

¼ cup diced yellow pepper

¼ cup finely minced carrot

½ cup finely chopped broccoli florets

1 teaspoon minced scallion

1 teaspoon chopped parsley

2 eggs, beaten

4 sole or flounder filets, 6-8 ounces each

1 cup flour

2 teaspoons vegetable oil

1 teaspoon butter

lemon wedges

1. Combine chopped vegetables together in a shallow pan

2. Crack the eggs and mix them well in a shallow pan.

3. Dredge the sole filets in flour, and then dip them in the eggs.

4. Shake off any excess egg, and then press the sole filets in the vegetable mix, coating both sides. The filets should be well coated with vegetables.

5. In a large skillet, heat 2 teaspoons of vegetable oil with a teaspoon of butter, and when sizzling hot, add the coated filets. Cook for 2 minutes, and then flip with a spatula, and cook on the other side. Squeeze a little lemon on the frying filets, remove from the skillet, and serve immediately.

SEA SCALLOPS WITH MCCOUN APPLES AND COCONUT MILK

Serves 4

The following recipe is the result of a bit of serendipity at a local farm stand. I had been purchasing apples with the intent of making applesauce, when the thought of combining sautéed sea scallops with apples struck me. McCoun apples are slightly sweet and firm, and work well in this recipe. The influences in this recipe are both New England and South Asian, and the blend of ginger, apples, and coconut milk is typical of much of the "fusion" cuisine of recent years. The richness of the coconut milk is more appealing in the cooler weather, and the addition of a few chilies will also help keep you warm.

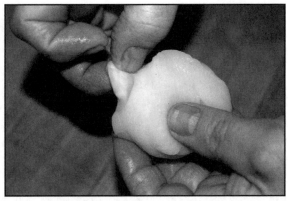

1. Clean the scallops by removing and discarding the tough muscle on the side.

2. Heat a large skillet with a little vegetable oil, and add the shallots and the scallops, ginger, red pepper, curry, crushed red pepper and the apples.

3. Stir well for about 2-3 minutes, and then add the coconut milk. Continue to cook for another minute, stirring well, while allowing the coconut milk to reduce.

4. Divide among 4 plates and serve over rice, and garnish with dry black currants.

2 pounds sea scallops

vegetable oil

1 teaspoon minced shallots

2 McCoun apples, thinly sliced

1 teaspoon minced fresh ginger

¼ teaspoon curry powder (optional)

dash crushed red pepper flakes

4 ounces canned coconut milk

1 julienne red pepper

2 cups cooked rice

1 tablespoon dried black currants

SEA SCALLOPS IN LEMONGRASS BROTH
Serves 4

Of all the food items grown in the garden, nothing is as different as growing your own lemongrass. If you buy lemongrass in the supermarket, it is generally dry and woody, almost like bamboo. Fresh lemongrass, however, is green and verdant, with a very powerful bouquet and flavor. The tops of the leaves are green like scallions, and full of flavor. The best way to use lemongrass is to make a broth, steeping the lemongrass in stock, sort of like tea. In colder weather, a hot well-seasoned broth is very appealing. The following recipe is the model of eastern simplicity; a few vegetables and fish in a pungent clear broth.

1 tablespoon minced shallot

1 teaspoon minced ginger

3 cups fish or chicken stock

2 stalks lemon-grass, chopped

2 tablespoons soy sauce

pinch crushed hot red pepper flakes

splash sherry

1 bunch scallion minced

1 red pepper, julienne

½ cup broccoli florets

1 pound sea scallops

1. In a small soup pot, brown the shallots and ginger, add the stock and lemongrass, pepper flakes, and soy sauce. Bring to a boil, then lower flame very low, cover, and let steep 30 minutes.

2. Strain the broth into a small saucepot, and then add the sherry.

3. Add the remaining ingredients into the strained broth, and simmer for 5 minutes.

4. Ladle into 4 bowls, and serve immediately.

POULTRY

Breast of Chicken with Braised Savoy Cabbage,
Mushrooms and Balsamic Glaze • 100

Roast Chicken • 101

Sesame Crusted Chicken Breast with
Braised Bok Choy and Ginger Sauce • 102

Breast of Chicken Poached in Plastic Wrap • 104

Breast of Chicken Stuffed with
Spinach and Portabella Mushrooms • 106

Breast of Chicken Stuffed with Berkshire Blue, Wrapped
with Prosciutto and Sage, Roasted Fig Sauce • 108

Chicken in Sweet Vermouth • 110

Breast of Chicken with Fava Beans • 112

Grilled Cornish Game Hen in Lemon,
Fennel and Garlic • 114

Breast of Duck with Black Currants,
Braised Apples and Pears • 115

Pan Fried Quail Stuffed with Couscous and Pine Nuts • 116

Warm Duck Salad with Crispy
Noodles and Cashews • 118

Breast of Duck with Braised Red Cabbage and Bacon • 120

Sautéed Pheasant with Chanterelles • 122

Apple Walnut Turkey Stuffing • 124

BREAST OF CHICKEN WITH BRAISED SAVOY CABBAGE, MUSHROOMS & BALSAMIC GLAZE

Serves 2

In the pantheon of vegetables, cabbage is surely one of the less appreciated. Asparagus, snap peas and fresh tomatoes are the "cool" vegetables. Cabbage clearly suffers from an inferiority complex, particularly in North America. The following recipe combines cabbage and shiitake mushrooms for a delicious autumn, woodsy flavor. The dill seed adds both flavor and texture. The sauce couldn't be simpler. By boiling down balsamic vinegar to a thick syrupy glaze, the result is the perfect foil for the cabbage.

2 cups balsamic vinegar

1 onion, peeled and sliced

olive oil

¼ pound shiitake mushrooms, stems removed, and sliced

½ head Savoy cabbage, thinly sliced

¼ teaspoon dill seed

1 bunch dill

2 breasts of chicken, fat trimmed, and cut in half

½ cup chicken stock

splash sherry wine vinegar

1. Preheat oven to 350°

2. In a stainless steel sauce pot, bring the balsamic vinegar to a boil and reduce by ¾, until the result is a thick syrup.

3. Brown the onions in a skillet, and add the mushrooms, cabbage, dill and dill seed. Lower the heat, toss well, let cook 2 minutes, and set aside.

4. In a separate large skillet, brown the chicken breasts on each side, and add the cooked cabbage mix into the pan. Place the skillet in the oven for 5 minutes.

5. Return the skillet to the stove top, add the chicken stock, and remove the chicken from the pan.

6. Place the cooked cabbage on 2 plates, and place the chicken on top.

7. Drizzle some balsamic glaze on top. Serve immediately.

ROAST CHICKEN

The more basic the recipe, the more important it is to use the highest quality ingredients. The key here is to use a high quality bird, preferably organic and cage free. The difference between a standard commercially raised chicken and cage-free organic one is enormous. The price difference is huge, too. Massaging the outside of the chicken with some soft butter yields both crisp skin and a rich flavor. The butter is balanced with a squeeze of lemon, and a few slivers of garlic and sprigs of fresh thyme provide the rest of the flavor.

1. Preheat the oven to 325°

2. Use a paring knife to create slits in the flesh of the chicken. Insert the slivered garlic into the openings created by the knife. Evenly distribute the garlic in the breast meat and legs.

3. Massage the butter evenly over the surface of the chicken.

4. Juice the lemon and pour over the top. Place the body of the lemon in the cavity of the chicken.

5. Place half of the thyme sprigs under the skin of the breast of the chicken, and put the remaining half of the thyme inside the cavity.

6. Place the chicken on a roasting pan, and roast for 1½ hours. Periodically baste the chicken with the pan drippings. Allow to rest for 15 minutes before attempting to carve.

7. Gravy can be made by scraping the pan drippings with a spatula or whisk, and adding either water or stock to the pan.

1 four to five-pound organic chicken

3 cloves garlic, peeled and slivered

4 tablespoons butter at room temperature

1 lemon

8 sprigs fresh thyme

SESAME CRUSTED CHICKEN BREAST WITH BRAISED BOK CHOY AND GINGER SAUCE

Serves 2

Sauce:

1 cup veal or chicken stock

⅓ cup hoisin sauce

1 tablespoon minced fresh ginger

Braised bok choy:

1 head bok choy

1 tablespoon sesame oil

4 boneless skinless chicken breasts

1 cup flour

2 eggs, beaten

2 cups sesame seeds

vegetable oil

½ cup minced scallions

A variation on breaded chicken breast is to coat the meat with a covering of sesame seeds. The result is a chewy, crunchy dish that makes for a substantial meal. It's a variation on the technique of first dipping the chicken in flour and then eggs, and instead of bread crumbs, the final coating is sesame seeds.

1. Preheat oven to 350°

2. To make the sauce, combine the stock, hoisin sauce and ginger, and simmer for 15 minutes, until reduced by ⅓.

3. Cut the bok choy into medium-sized chunks, and wash carefully.

4. Heat a little sesame oil in a skillet or wok, and sauté the bok choy for a minute. Add ½ the sauce into the pan, and cook for another minute. Set aside.

5. Trim the breasts of any excess fat, and use a meat mallet to evenly pound and flatten out the flesh.

6. First dip the breasts in flour, then in the beaten eggs, and finally in the sesame seeds.

7. Heat a little vegetable oil in a heavy bottomed skillet and brown the chicken on each side for about 2 minutes. Then place the skillet in the oven for about 4 minutes.

8. Place the cooked bok choy on 2 plates, and place the cooked chicken on top.

9. Ladle the remaining sauce on top, and garnish with scallions.

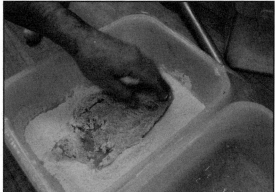

BREAST OF CHICKEN POACHED IN PLASTIC WRAP
Serves 4

One of the most common New Year's resolutions is to try and lose weight and reduce fat intake, and the following recipe for breast of chicken poached in plastic wrap contains virtually no fat at all. At first the idea seems unbelievable, but you can wrap a breast of chicken in plastic wrap and poach it in boiling water, thus eliminating any of the fat involved in sautéing or grilling. The chicken cooks quickly, and after removing the plastic bundle from the water, unwrap the chicken and slice the meat into discs to reveal the colorful stuffing inside. The plastic keeps the meat moist, and the result is tasty and low in fat.

4 boneless, skinless chicken breasts

1 leek, thinly sliced

1 red pepper, thinly sliced

1 carrot, thinly sliced

1 bunch chives

pinch salt and pepper

fresh thyme

1. Remove any fat from the chicken, and using a meat mallet, pound the chicken into a uniformly thin piece.

2. Cut the vegetables into thin, matchstick size pieces, and combine them together in a bowl with remaining ingredients, and toss.

3. Place a piece of plastic wrap about 18" long on the counter and place a pounded chicken breast in the center.

4. Place a small mound of the sliced vegetables on the chicken breast and roll the chicken tightly around the vegetables so as to enclose them with the meat.

5. Roll up the entire chicken breast in the plastic wrap, and holding the two ends of the plastic in each hand, twist the wrap tightly so the chicken bundle is tightly enclosed in the plastic. Tie the two ends together to prevent them from unwrapping.

6. Drop the plastic bundle in some gently boiling water for about 8 minutes, and when finished cooking remove from the water with a slotted spoon.

7. Carefully remove the plastic wrap, and use a serrated knife to slice the meat into discs. Serve with a highly seasoned tomato sauce, or a sauce made from reducing stock.

BREAST OF CHICKEN STUFFED WITH SPINACH AND PORTABELLA MUSHROOMS

Serves 4

There are several ways to stuff a breast of chicken, but the method I use most often is to clean each half and pound it thinly with a meat mallet, which creates a large thin piece suitable for stuffing. For the following recipe the spinach is chopped coarsely, used raw, combined with a mixture of roasted portabella mushrooms and onions, and bound with a little egg and breadcrumbs. Roasting the portabellas first removes the excess water in them, and makes for a more attractive filling. Once the breasts are stuffed, they can be browned quickly in a sauté pan, and finished in an oven in just minutes. Slicing them in half before serving reveals a colorful and verdant interior.

4 whole boneless, skinless chicken breasts

olive oil

1 Spanish onion, diced

4 portabella mushrooms

1 pound raw spinach, cleaned and chopped coarsely

1 egg

½ cup breadcrumbs

fresh thyme

salt and pepper

1. Preheat oven to 350°

2. Remove the center membrane from the chicken breast and any fat from the edges, and cut in half down the center. Use a meat mallet to pound each ½ breast into a large, uniformly thin piece.

3. Sauté the onion in a skillet in a little oil until well browned, and reserve until cool.

4. Discard the stems from the portabellas, and roast the caps for about 15 minutes, until well cooked. When cool, dice into small pieces.

5. To make the stuffing, remove the stems from the spinach, wash and dry well, and then coarsely chop. Combine the sautéed onion, mushrooms and chopped spinach in a mixing bowl. Add the egg and breadcrumbs, season with salt, pepper and fresh thyme, and mix well.

6. Place a small mound of the stuffing in the center of each flattened out chicken breast, and roll up each piece, placing seam side down.

7. Heat a large skillet with a little oil and brown the stuffed breasts for about 2 minutes on each side. Transfer the skillet to the oven and cook for another 10 minutes.

8. Remove the skillet from the oven. Slice each stuffed breast in half, to reveal the stuffing, and place the sliced, stuffed breasts on each dinner plate. Serve immediately.

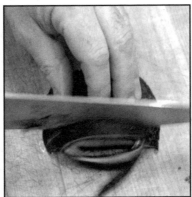

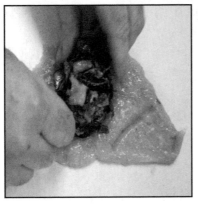

BREAST OF CHICKEN STUFFED WITH BERKSHIRE BLUE, WRAPPED WITH PROSCIUTTO AND SAGE, ROASTED FIG SAUCE

Serves 4

One of the all time classic food combinations is prosciutto, sage, blue cheese and figs. All these flavors are combined in a stuffed chicken breast to make a delicious and sophisticated dish, yet one that is not hard to make. Either fresh or roasted figs can be used in this recipe. It does take dexterity to wrap the chicken with the prosciutto and sage, but, like everything else, practice makes perfect. Even after being sautéed and baked, the sage leaf retains its vibrant green color. The flavors in this recipe are classically Italian, although I use the locally produced, and very creamy, Berkshire Blue, instead of Gorgonzola.

4 boneless, skinless chicken breasts

8 thin slices of Berkshire Blue cheese (or other blue cheese)

8 thin slices of prosciutto

8 fresh sage leaves

olive oil

1. Preheat oven to 350°

2. Trim any fat off the chicken breasts, and remove the center membrane.

3. Using a meat mallet, carefully pound the breasts to flatten them out.

4. Place a small piece of blue cheese in the center of the flattened breast, and roll up.

5. Place a sage leaf on top of the chicken breasts, and tightly wrap a piece of the prosciutto around the leaf and the chicken.

6. Heat a skillet with a little olive oil and brown the stuffed chicken on all sides.

7. Place the skillet in the oven for about 8 minutes.

8. Remove from the oven, and serve with fig sauce.

Fig Sauce:

1. Combine the demi-glacé with the vinegar in a small sauce pot.

2. Add the roasted or fresh figs, and simmer for 5 minutes. Serve over the chicken.

Fig sauce:

1 cup demi-glacé (see page 185)

splash fig vinegar

¼ cup roasted or fresh figs

CHICKEN IN SWEET VERMOUTH

Serves 4

The classic French version of coq au vin uses dry red wine in which to braise the chicken, typically a Burgundy, Beaujolais or Rhône wine. Local chefs are partial to the wine of their particular region, and will argue that their rendition is the truest or most authentic version. And while chicken braised in dry red wine is delicious, using a sweeter wine like red vermouth gives a very different flavor, and one I enjoy. It's just another variation on coq au vin. You can't be stingy with the wine. The chicken must be almost completely submerged in the wine, so it will certainly require at least one full bottle to cook a chicken. The alcohol cooks off almost completely, so you needn't be concerned about getting hung over from this dish. What remains is the pleasantly sweet taste of the wine, which makes for a moist and hearty dinner.

1 Spanish onion (or pearl onions)

olive oil or butter

1 whole chicken, cut in quarters

2 large carrots

1 tablespoon minced garlic

1 bottle sweet vermouth (750 ml)

bay leaf

salt and pepper

cornstarch (optional)

1. Preheat oven to 350°

2. In a heavy-bottomed casserole dish, lightly brown the onion in a little olive oil or butter. Cook over medium heat until golden.

3. Season the chicken with salt and pepper and add it, skin side down, and brown for about 2 minutes on each side.

4. Add the carrot and garlic, salt and pepper, and stir and brown for 1 minute.

5. Add the vermouth, and cover the pot with a lid

6. Bake for about 1 hour.

110

7. Remove the chicken and vegetables from the pot with a slotted spoon. Skim off any fat or grease from the top of the sauce. If you prefer a thicker sauce, dissolve about 2 teaspoons of cornstarch in a little cold water, and stir it into the sauce and heat until the sauce thickens. Serve with couscous or mashed potatoes.

BREAST OF CHICKEN WITH FAVA BEANS

Serves 4

Fava beans are enjoying a current popularity with cutting edge chefs at many leading restaurants, even though they are known as an ingredient in "peasant" food. They are not widely eaten in America, in part because they require a lot of work to prepare. Too many people only know fava beans as the subject of a joke by the fictional Hannibal Lechter in *The Silence of the Lambs*. First you must shell the beans from their pods, and then blanch the bean, and finally peel off the fibrous and tough outer layer. This yields a tender light green bean, which is soft and delicious, and which can be eaten as is, in a sautéed dish, or puréed into a sauce. However, by the time you shell the beans and peel the outer layer off, what started out as a quart of pods yields barely half a cup of tender beans. The following recipe for a thinly pounded breast of chicken with fava beans can be prepared relatively quickly once the beans are shelled and blanched.

1 cup peeled, blanched, fava beans

olive oil

4 boneless skinless chicken breasts, thinly pounded

½ teaspoon minced garlic

½ teaspoon capers

½ cup peeled diced tomatoes

1 cup white wine

1. Remove the beans from their pods, blanch them in boiling water for 30 seconds, and peel off the tough, fibrous outer layer.

2. Heat a little olive oil in a large skillet, and when very hot, add the thinly pounded chicken breasts. Cook for 2 minutes on one side, and then turn over.

3. Add the garlic and fava beans, cook an additional 2 minutes, then add the white wine, chopped tomatoes and capers.

4. Allow the wine to reduce by ⅔, remove the chicken from the pan, and place on four plates. Pour some of the sauce on top of each piece of chicken, and serve immediately.

Preparing fava beans is a time-consuming labor of love. First you must shell them like garden peas, then blanch them in boiling water for a minute. Finally, their outer skin must be peeled and discarded, revealing a tiny, bright green soft pea in the center. But it is worth the effort.

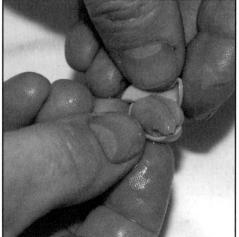

GRILLED CORNISH GAME HEN IN LEMON, FENNEL AND GARLIC
Serves 4

The proverb about good things coming in small packages applies to food as well. Rather than just grilling pieces of chicken, which have been cut into pieces, there is something nice about serving guests their own individual package of grilled food. A Cornish game hen serves one, and can be easily cooked on the grill by removing the backbone. It helps to marinate the bird for at least several hours or overnight. The flavors of lemon, fennel, and garlic combine to create a light but savory seasoning. A spice or coffee grinder can be used to grind the fennel seeds, which are both fragrant and potent.

4 Cornish game hens

juice and zest of 1 lemon

½ cup vegetable oil

1 tablespoon minced garlic

1 teaspoon fennel seeds, finely ground

1. Trim off the ends of the wing joints, and reserve for making stock.

2. To remove the backbone, insert a small boning knife into the cavity of the bird, and separate the thigh joint from the backbone on each side of the bird's spine. The entire backbone should come out in one piece. Flatten the bird with the palm of your hand, to make grilling easier.

3. Combine the zest and juice of 1 lemon with the oil, garlic and ground fennel seed, and marinate the hens for at least a few hours or overnight.

4. Remove the hens from the marinade, and grill for about 10-12 minutes on each side, until done. To test for doneness, insert a knife into the leg joint. When the juices run clear, the hen is cooked. Serve hot.

BREAST OF DUCK WITH BLACK CURRANTS, BRAISED APPLES AND PEARS

Serves 4

There is something about the change in the weather and cooler nights that makes cooking with apples appealing. The following recipe for breast of duck calls for the meat to be served with a combination of braised apples and pears. The trick is to cook the fruit enough so that it is soft, but not mushy. The natural sweetness of the apples compliments the duck. Cooking boneless duck breast is much easier than preparing a whole duck, and requires much less time.

1. Preheat oven to 400°

2. Core and cut the pears and apples without peeling them. In a large skillet, heat a little butter. Add the Granny Smith and pear, and sauté over low heat for about 5 minutes. Add the Macintosh apples, which need less cooking. Add the nutmeg and currants and continue to cook and stir for about 5 minutes. Add the brandy, and ignite with a match so that it flames. Remove from the heat.

3. In another large skillet, cook the duck breast, skin side down, for about 3 minutes, then flip over, and place the skillet in the oven for 5 minutes.

4. Remove the duck from the oven and carve the meat into thin slices. Heat up the apple and pear mix, and mound some of the fruit on the center of 4 plates. Arrange the meat around the fruit. Serve warm.

2 Macintosh apples

1 Bosc pear

1 Granny Smith apple

butter

2 tablespoons dried currants

dash nutmeg

splash brandy

4 duck breasts, 6-8 ounces each

PAN FRIED QUAIL STUFFED WITH COUSCOUS & PINE NUTS
Serves 4

While once limited to the tables of fine restaurants and gourmets, quail are now readily available in good butcher shops, and are really quite easy to prepare. Just because they are small is no reason to be intimidated. Quail can be purchased partially boned and ready for grilling, or whole. Depending on the recipe, you may prefer one or the other. The following recipe for quail stuffed with couscous and toasted pine nuts uses the whole quail. Browned in a skillet and then finished in the oven, the whole cooking process takes only about 12-15 minutes. Served on a bed of wilted spinach, this makes a great meal for a special occasion.

8 whole quail

salt

2 cups prepared couscous

¼ cup toasted pine nuts

¼ cup dry black currants

½ red onion, minced

½ red bell pepper, minced

flour

olive oil

1 pound fresh spinach, cleaned

1. Preheat oven to 400°

2. Wash out the center cavity of the quail, and lightly salt.

3. In a small bowl, combine the prepared couscous with the toasted nuts, currants, red onion and pepper, and mix well.

4. Stuff the cavity of the birds with the couscous mix.

5. Dredge the birds lightly in flour and brown, using olive oil, in a large skillet for about 2 minutes on each side, turning the birds carefully.

6. Place the skillet in the oven, and roast for about 10 minutes.

7. Remove the skillet from the oven, take the quail and transfer to a platter. Quickly sauté the spinach in the hot pan for about one minute. The goal is to lightly cook the spinach without having it get overcooked and soupy.

8. Place the wilted spinach on the bottom of 4 plates, and put the quail on top of the spinach. Serve immediately.

WARM DUCK SALAD WITH CRISPY NOODLES AND CASHEWS

Serves 4

Duck has a natural affinity for things both sweet and crunchy, which is featured in the following recipe for warm duck salad. The sweet comes in the form of an unusual soy sauce from Indonesia, where a thicker, sweeter version of soy sauce, almost the consistency of molasses, provides just the right amount of sweetness. The crunch comes from lightly toasted cashews, deep fried noodles, and a discreet quantity of shredded iceberg lettuce mixed into the salad greens. Some foodies may be surprised or even alarmed at the use of iceberg lettuce mixed with mesclun greens, but the proof is in the salad.

1 cup fried noodles

Dressing:

1 cup vegetable oil

⅓ cup rice wine vinegar

1 teaspoon Dijon mustard

1 tablespoon minced fresh ginger

⅓ cup ABC Indonesian sweet soy sauce

4 boneless duck breasts, 6-8 ounces each

4 cups mesclun lettuce

½ head iceberg lettuce, shredded

2 ribs celery, in small pieces

1 julienne red pepper

½ cup lightly toasted cashews

1. Preheat oven to 400°

2. To make the noodles, deep fry some linguini or spaghetti (leftovers are fine) in hot oil for about 2 minutes until crispy. Drain well.

3. To make the dressing, combine the ingredients in a glass jar and shake well.

4. To cook the duck, heat a skillet very, very hot without any oil at all, and place the duck breasts skin side down. The skin contains sufficient fat to fry the duck. Cook for 2 minutes skin side down, turn over, and cook 2 more minutes. Then place skillet in the oven for 5 minutes.

5. Remove duck from oven after 5 minutes, and set aside.

6. In a large salad bowl, combine the shredded iceberg, mesclun lettuce, celery, red peppers and dressing. Divide dressed greens among 4 plates.

7. Using a very sharp knife, carve the duck breasts into thin slices, and arrange around plates. Ring the perimeter of the plates with the fried noodles and sprinkle toasted cashews on top. Serve immediately.

BREAST OF DUCK WITH BRAISED RED CABBAGE AND BACON

Serves 4

There are some vegetables that are very popular and trendy, and which frequently appear on restaurant menus. Asparagus, mesclun salad, wild mushrooms and baby vegetables might be included on this list. Other vegetables are perennially ignored, and they require a certain amount of affirmative action by chefs and food writers. Kohlrabi, rutabagas, beets and red cabbage are certainly members of this latter group. There is a vast swath of Central Europe where eating red cabbage is more common than in America, and in these parts the locals know how delicious and hearty it can be during long, cold winters. But here in America, red cabbage scarcely ever makes an appearance except as a garnish in coleslaw. In an effort to address this glaring oversight, I offer the following recipe for breast of duck with red cabbage. The vinegar in the cabbage offsets the richness and fat in the duck.

1 head red cabbage,
finely shredded

½ pound slab bacon,
cut into cubes

1 Spanish onion,
thinly sliced

1 teaspoon caraway seeds

¼ cup vinegar (red wine,
raspberry, or balsamic)

¼ cup dry black currants

2 cups stock
(chicken or beef)

4 boneless duck breasts,
6-8 ounces each

salt and pepper

1. Preheat oven to 400°

2. Remove the tough outer leaves of the cabbage, and discard. Cut the cabbage in half, remove the tough stem and core, and cut or shred finely.

3. In a heavy bottomed skillet or casserole, brown the bacon until well cooked and the fat is rendered.

4. Remove the cooked bacon with a slotted spoon and brown onions in the bacon fat until golden brown, and then add the cabbage.

5. Over moderate heat, stir cabbage well for about 5 minutes, and then add the caraway seeds, currants, vinegar, cooked bacon, and stock.

6. Cover the casserole, and let the cabbage simmer slowly over low heat for about 15-20 minutes. Test for doneness; the cabbage should be soft. Taste for salt and pepper.

7. To prepare the duck breast, heat a skillet very hot without any oil or butter at all; place the breast in the skillet skin side down, and brown for 2 minutes. Turn over and brown for another 2 minutes.

8. Place the skillet with the duck breast in the oven for about 5 minutes to finish cooking.

9. Remove from the oven, and carve the duck into thin slices.

10. To serve, place a mound of the warm red cabbage in the center of 4 plates and arrange the sliced duck breast on top. Serve immediately.

SAUTÉED PHEASANT WITH CHANTERELLES
Serves 4

The idea of preparing pheasant may seem intimidating and too ambitious for the average home cook, but a pheasant is just a bird like any other, and if you can cook chicken, you can prepare quail, squab or pheasant. However, you will have to spend a little more money, because game birds are more expensive. Pheasant are farm raised, and are available in 1-pound size, which is about the same size as a Cornish hen, and perfect for 1 serving. Because pheasant are very lean, they benefit from cooking in a liquid after being browned in a skillet. This keeps the meat from drying out. The addition of some wild mushrooms, and fortified wine like Madeira or port transforms the dish into something truly special, yet well within the repertoire of a modestly skilled cook. If chanterelles aren't available, shiitakes may be substituted.

4 one-pound pheasants

flour

butter or olive oil

½ pound chanterelles or other wild mushrooms

1 tablespoon minced shallot

1 teaspoon fresh chopped thyme

½ cup peeled, seeded diced tomatoes

1 cup chicken or veal stock

½ cup Madeira or port

salt and pepper

1. Preheat oven to 400°

2. Remove the wing joints from the bird, and save for stock. To remove the backbone, insert a sharp boning knife into the cavity of the bird and cut along both sides of the backbone, which is on the bottom of the bird when sitting breast side up on a cutting board. Remove the breast meat from the frame of the bird by running your boning knife close to the bone. You should end up with 2 boned-out breasts and 2 leg-thigh pieces.

3. Lightly dredge the bird in flour and brown in a little olive oil or butter with the shallots and mushrooms. Season with salt and pepper and brown on each side for 2 minutes. Add the fresh thyme, tomatoes, stock and wine, cover the pan and place in the oven for 10 minutes.

4. Remove the skillet from the oven, and remove the pheasant from the pan. Place the skillet on top of the stove, and reduce the liquid by half. Place the pheasant on 4 plates, and ladle the sauce over the top.

APPLE WALNUT TURKEY STUFFING

For a 20 Pound Turkey

Ask a dozen chefs, and you will get a dozen different answers as to what they think is the ideal turkey stuffing. Frankly I've never understood what an oyster is supposed to be doing inside a turkey, as some traditionalists stuff their birds. And sausage seems to be an addition of an unnecessary meat into a meal which is already too big. I've always felt the relatively simpler the better when it comes to turkey stuffing. The most important attribute of stuffing is that it be moist, and the apples in the following recipe do just that. It isn't stuffing unless it's cooked inside the bird, and don't let the health police dissuade you from cooking it inside the turkey. Simply be sure not to stuff the bird until immediately before roasting.

2 large onions, peeled and thinly sliced

butter or oil

1 head of celery, finely chopped

4 carrots, peeled and diced

6 Granny Smith apples, cored, diced and peeled

1 cup walnuts, coarsely chopped

splash brandy

6 cups seasoned bread croutons

6 eggs, beaten

½ stick melted butter

2 tablespoons sage

1 teaspoon fresh thyme

salt and pepper

1. In a large skillet, brown the onions in a little butter or oil, and when lightly browned, add the carrots and celery.

2. Remove the vegetables from the skillet, and let cool. Lightly brown the apples in a little oil or butter, and deglaze with a little brandy.

3. Allow the apples and vegetables to cool; then combine them in a large mixing bowl with the croutons, walnuts, eggs, and the seasonings. Pour the melted butter over the mix, and stir well.

4. The stuffing can be made up to a day in advance, but don't stuff the bird until just before putting it in the oven.

MEAT

POT ROAST
Serves 8

When it comes to comfort food, pot roast is at the top of the list. It's the kind of food that people typically associate with home cooking, and it is not often seen on restaurant menus. That's a shame, because a well-made pot roast is a delicious meal. Even people who are not vegetable eaters find it hard to resist a tender carrot cooked in the gravy. It's essential to make the pot roast the day before, and then chill it after cooking. The meat should be sliced as thin as possible, and that can only be done when the meat is cold. Simply reheat the sliced meat in the cooking liquid.

1 six to seven-pound beef bottom round

2 Spanish onions, sliced

3 carrots, chopped

3 potatoes, cut into large chunks

1 teaspoon dry thyme

2 bay leaves

2 quarts beef stock

1 cup Marsala or port

½ cup ketchup

salt and pepper

1. Preheat oven to 325°

2. Trim any sinew off the meat, and season with salt and pepper.

3. In a heavy-bottomed pot, brown the meat on all sides, for about 5 minutes.

4. Remove the meat from the pot, and brown the onions, adding the thyme and bay leaves.

5. Return the beef to the pot, add the carrots, potatoes, ketchup, Marsala, and then cover with the stock.

6. Place a lid lightly on the pot and put it in the oven for 3 hours.

7. Remove the pot from oven and remove the meat from the pot.

8. Put the meat in the refrigerator and let chill overnight. When cooled down, refrigerate the sauce and vegetables as well.

9. The next day, slice the meat as thinly as possible, and heat up in the pot with the sauce and vegetables.

126

VEAL SCALOPPINI WITH LAVENDER
Serves 4

One of the oldest culinary truisms is that smell precedes taste. Before you eat most foods, you can smell them. That is what is so great about walking into a kitchen with the smell of bread baking, chocolate melting, or roasts roasting. One herb that is extremely aromatic, but is more often thought of as a cosmetic fragrance than a cooking herb, is lavender. The smell is powerful and unmistakable. The green leaves look like pine needles or rosemary, and they, rather then the purple flower, are what can be used to season food. A little goes a long way, and frequently lavender is combined with thyme and rosemary and is sometimes referred to as "herbes de Provence." When the lavender is in blossom in the south of France it is one of the world's greatest spectacles. A pinch of lavender in coq au vin, braised meats and game adds an exotic flavor.

12 pieces of veal scaloppini, pounded thin

flour

¼ cup vegetable oil

2 shallots, minced

¼ pounds shiitake or wild mushrooms

⅓ teaspoon minced fresh lavender

¼ cup Madeira or port

salt and pepper

1. Lightly flour the veal, and in a hot skillet, brown it for about 1 minute on each side.

2. Remove the meat from the pan, add a little more oil, sauté the shallots and mushrooms together and add the lavender. Season with salt and pepper.

3. Let cook 1 minute, add the Madeira or port, and place the veal back in the pan with the sauce and mushrooms.

4. Let cook for about 1 minute or until the sauce thickens slightly. Serve immediately.

PORK LOIN STUFFED WITH APRICOTS

Serves 6-8

One of the classic food combinations is that of pork with dried fruit such as apricots or prunes. A pork loin is easy to stuff, and inexpensive, but can make for an impressive main course with the addition of a colorful and savory stuffing. Have your butcher remove the bones, and then butterfly the loin, which makes a vehicle for stuffing. The addition of apples and raisins provides both moisture and flavor. This dish can be enjoyed hot out of the oven or served cold as a variation on paté.

⅓ of a boneless pork loin roast (about 4 pounds)

2 Granny Smith apples, peeled and diced

butter

2 thumb-sized pieces of ginger, finely minced

½ cup dried apricots

½ cup raisins

brandy

butcher's twine

1. Preheat oven to 350°

2. To prepare the meat, butterfly the filet, and using a meat mallet, lightly pound the meat to flatten it out.

3. Sauté the peeled apples in a little butter, deglaze with a little brandy, and let cool.

4. Spread the minced ginger over the inside of the pork loin. Spread the apples, apricots and raisins over the center of the meat, and roll up like a jellyroll, as tightly as possible. Use some butcher's twine to tie the meat into a bundle.

5. Roast for about 1 hour. Serve either hot or chilled.

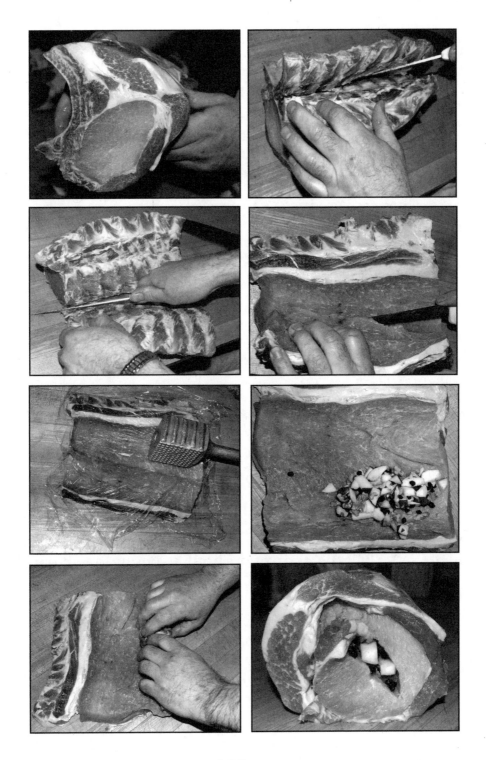

129

GRILLED PORK CHOPS
WITH CRUSHED CUMIN SEED
Serves 2

The difference in flavor between standard, commercially raised pork and that of organically raised, Heritage Breed meat is profound. While conventional modern industrial agriculture raises only a very limited number of livestock breeds, the Heritage Breed movement is attempting to preserve a wide variety of livestock breeds, many of which have become endangered. Americans are accustomed to equating size with quality, and that is not always the case in the food world. As a rule, organically raised meat, which is hormone free, is smaller in size, but more delicately flavored. This meat is so tasty that it doesn't make sense to mask it with a heavy marinade or sauce. A simple coating of garlic, and coarsely ground cumin seeds and black peppercorns is all that is required.

½ teaspoon
cumin seeds

½ teaspoon
whole black
peppercorns

4 six-ounce
loin pork chops

1 teaspoon
minced garlic

1 teaspoon
vegetable oil

1. Use the edge of a heavy skillet on a hard work surface to crush the cumin seeds and peppercorns.

2. Combine the pork chops with the crushed spices, garlic and oil in a small bowl and toss to coat and season.

3. Grill the chops for about 3-4 minutes on each side on a hot grill, and serve immediately.

PORK TENDERLOIN WITH BLACK-EYED PEAS, ROASTED GARLIC SAUCE

Serves 4

Black-eyed peas are a favorite below the Mason Dixon, but they're not often served up north. That's a shame because they are delicious, and they are a particularly good accompaniment to pork. As any good Southerner knows, good bacon is an essential ingredient in making these peas, and a heavily smoked piece of slab bacon is the best. Allow the peas to cook slowly and absorb all the flavors.

1. Preheat oven to 350°

2. Soak the peas in water overnight, and then cook for about an hour. When soft, drain the peas.

3. In a heavy-bottomed sauce pan, cook the bacon until it yields a little fat and then add the onion. Cook the bacon and onion together over moderate heat until well browned. Add the garlic, tomatoes, and pepper flakes if using, and cook slowly for about 20-30 minutes. Add a little water to moisten the peas periodically if they get too dry.

4. Brown the pork tenderloin in a skillet on top of the stove, and season well on all sides. Place the skillet in the oven for about 5 minutes to finish cooking.

5. To serve, place a mound of peas in the center of 4 plates. Slice the pork tenderloin into thin discs, and place them around the plate. Serve with Roasted Garlic Sauce (see page 182).

1 pound dry black-eyed peas

½ pound slab bacon, cut into cubes

1 Spanish onion, chopped

1 teaspoon minced garlic

½ cup peeled diced tomatoes

dash dry red pepper flakes (optional)

2 pork tenderloins

ROAST LEG OF LAMB
Serves 8-10

Cooking a large roast is both simple and festive, and certainly meets the requirements of a holiday meal. A leg of lamb, especially one boned out by your butcher, can be well seasoned inside the cavity as well as outside, and then simply placed in the oven without any other fuss. A lamb leg is also much more affordable than either rib or loin chops. It will serve about 10 people. Any roast can be removed from the oven when about 90% cooked, and then left to sit on top of the oven well covered for up to 2 hours, before carving. This allows you to spend time with family and friends instead of being tied up in the kitchen.

1. Preheat oven to 375°

1 leg of lamb, boned

2 tablespoons minced garlic

2 tablespoons minced fresh rosemary

1 tablespoon olive oil

1 tablespoon balsamic vinegar

salt and pepper

2. Have your butcher remove the bone from a leg of lamb. This will make for faster cooking and easier carving. In addition, with the bone removed the inside cavity of the meat can be more easily seasoned.

3. Combine the garlic, rosemary, oil and vinegar into a slurry or paste and spread inside the lamb as well as outside.

4. Place the meat in a roasting pan, and bake for about 1¼-1½ hours, depending on the size of the leg.

5. Remove the roast from the oven, and allow at least 15 minutes for the juices to settle before carving.

LAMB "SCALOPPINI" WITH ROASTED EGGPLANT
Serves 8

While it is common to eat slices of veal that have been pounded into paper thin pieces, and sometimes called scaloppini, it is less common to eat lamb that way. There's no real reason for the popularity of veal over lamb, and you can prepare lamb the same way. When preparing either veal or lamb, the meat from the leg can be used, which is a more affordable cut. Pounding the meat with a mallet both tenderizes the meat and allows you to cook it in just minutes, as opposed to the hours it would take to roast a leg of lamb. Your butcher can assist by removing the bone. And while they are not commonly served together, lamb and roasted eggplant, or baba ghanouj, are a terrific flavor combination, as the following recipe reveals.

1. Preheat oven to 300°

2. Trim the meat of any sinew, cut into thin slices and place in between 2 sheets of plastic wrap. Use a meat mallet to pound into uniformly thin slices.

3. To make the sauce, drizzle a little olive oil over the eggplant and bake for 1 hour. Turn the eggplant over once while baking. It will collapse and be soft when cooked.

4. When cool, cut the eggplant in half, remove the soft pulp from the inside, and discard the skin.

5. Place the eggplant with the remaining sauce ingredients in a food processor, and purée.

1 leg of lamb, boned out (this will provide enough meat for at least 8 servings)

olive oil

1 teaspoon minced shallot

½ teaspoon minced fresh rosemary

For the sauce:

2 whole eggplant

2 tablespoons tahini

1 bunch parsley, washed

½ teaspoon minced garlic

juice 1 lemon

2 tablespoons olive oil

133

6. Final assembly: heat a little olive oil in a large skillet, brown the lamb pieces on each side for 2 minutes, seasoning with the shallots and rosemary.

7. Remove the lamb from the pan. Put the eggplant purée in the pan for just 1 minute to warm it up.

8. Spread the eggplant purée on the bottom of the serving plates and place the lamb pieces on top. Serve immediately.

CASSOULET OF LAMB

Serves 4

In the dead of winter, one sure way to keep warm is to eat hearty food, like cassoulet. Cassoulet is the classic French dish of white beans, sausage, and duck or lamb, and there are many regional variations on the theme. Most are made with confit of duck, but the following recipe is made with braised lamb shank and traditional garlic sausage. Lamb shanks are one of the least expensive cuts, yet after several hours braising they are very flavorful and tender

1. Preheat oven to 400°

2. In a heavy-bottomed saucepan, brown the bacon until it is cooked and has rendered its fat.

3. Add the shanks to the pan, season with salt and pepper and half of the rosemary, and brown for 2 minutes on each side.

4. Add the carrots and onions and the remaining rosemary, brown the vegetables for 2 minutes, and then add the garlic.

5. Add the stock, so that the shanks are submerged in liquid, and add the sausage. Cover tightly. Cook for 3 to 3½ hours. The shank meat should easily separate from the bone when done.

6. To serve, either pack individual small casserole dishes with a shank, some of the white beans, sausage and sauce, or alternatively, to serve family style, add some of the precooked white beans directly into the casserole after 2½ hours of cooking, and serve directly out of the casserole, ladling some of the meat, beans, sausage and sauce onto each plate.

¼ pound bacon lardons

4 lamb shanks

salt and pepper

1 tablespoon chopped fresh rosemary

1 onion, sliced

2 carrots, diced

1 tablespoon minced garlic

1 pound garlic sausage

1 quart beef, veal, or lamb stock (water, if no stock available)

2 cups cooked Great Northern or cannelini beans

STEAK AU POIVRE
Serves 2

Although the supply is very limited, the Castle Street Café is fortunate to be able to serve grass-fed, locally raised natural beef, from Foggy River Farm in Great Barrington and Moon in the Pond Farm in Sheffield. Even in the dead of winter it is possible to eat locally grown. The following recipe for steak au poivre can be made with a variety of steak cuts, including New York strip steaks, eye round or even filet. If you're able to obtain locally raised grass-fed beef, so much the better.

2 ten-ounce steaks

1 tablespoon black pep-percorns

splash brandy or cognac

1 cup veal stock

1. Preheat oven to 375°

2. Trim away any excess fat from the steaks, and use a meat mallet to pound and tenderize.

3. Crush the peppercorns, using the bottom of a skillet to drag and press them. They should be very coarsely crushed.

4. Press one side of the steak into the crushed peppercorns, and place the steak, peppercorn side down, in a hot skillet.

5. Cook the steak for about 2 minutes on each side, deglaze the pan with a splash of brandy, and add the veal stock to the pan.

6. Place the skillet in the oven for about 2 minutes, depending on its thickness. The steak will be rare after about 2 minutes.

7. Remove the skillet from the stove, check for doneness, remove the steak from the pan and pour the sauce over the steak. Serve immediately.

There is a tremendous difference between locally raised grass-fed beef and standard commercial beef. Grass-fed beef is much leaner, and this means that it is better suited for some uses than others. Grass-fed beef tends to make for a dry and crumbly hamburger, but it works well for meatloaf and for making meat sauce for pasta. Meatloaf makes a satisfying and unpretentious meal. It is not that different from paté. It also makes for a great cold sandwich, which somehow always tastes better made standing in front of the fridge late at night.

1. Preheat oven to 325°

2. In the bowl of an electric mixer, combine all the ingredients, using only half of the ketchup.

3. Mix at low speed for one minute. Be careful not to overmix, or the meat will become tough.

4. Form the meat into a long loaf on a baking pan.

5. Spread the reserved ½ cup of ketchup on top of the loaf.

6. Bake for 40 minutes. Serve hot or cold.

3 pounds ground beef

1 onion, puréed

½ teaspoon salt

½ teaspoon ground black pepper

6 eggs

1 cup breadcrumbs

1 teaspoon dry basil

1 teaspoon dry thyme

1 cup ketchup

BALSAMIC AND ROSEMARY MARINATED FILET MIGNON

Serves 4

The arrival of real spring weather and the full blossoming of the trees signify the beginning of outdoor grilling season in earnest. When the days start growing longer, and it is warm enough to eat outdoors, who wants to spend time cooking indoors? The following recipe for balsamic vinegar and rosemary marinade is delicious on either beef or lamb. The key to this is using fresh rosemary; the dried version is not worth using.

4 filet mignon steaks, 6-8 ounces each

1 cup balsamic vinegar

2 cups vegetable oil

2 tablespoons minced garlic

1 tablespoon finely minced fresh rosemary

freshly ground black pepper

1. Have your butcher trim and prepare the filet steaks.

2. In a small stainless bowl, whisk together the vinegar, garlic and rosemary, and then whisk in the oil. Add fresh pepper to taste.

3. Add the beef to the marinade for at least 2 hours, or as much as several days. The longer the beef marinates, the stronger the flavor.

4. To cook, remove the beef from the marinade and grill over high heat until cooked as you like. Serve immediately.

Making short ribs is a good way to illustrate the difference between commercially raised beef and grass-fed beef. Short ribs made from standard commercial beef tend to be very fatty, and when fully cooked the ribs often sit in a lot of rendered grease, which must be strained off. Grass-fed beef is much leaner, and short ribs made from them are much less greasy, while just as tender. It's a great meal for a cold winter night. The trick is to cook the meat enough so that it is tender, but not so much that the meat falls off the rib bone. It helps to place the ribs bone side down when in the oven.

1. Preheat oven to 400°

2. Season the ribs with salt and pepper and place them bone side down in a shallow pan; one just deep enough to hold the meat.

3. In a large skillet, sauté the onion until golden, then add the garlic, diced tomatoes and thyme.

4. Pour the onion and tomato mix over the ribs, and add the diced carrots.

5. Cover the ribs with beef broth.

6. Cover the pan tightly with a lid or aluminum foil, and bake for 2 hours.

7. Remove from the oven and skim off any grease that may have formed on top. Serve with mashed potatoes or couscous.

4 pounds short ribs

1 Spanish onion, peeled and sliced

1 teaspoon minced garlic

½ teaspoon chopped fresh thyme

4 carrots, peeled and diced

1 cup peeled diced tomatoes

4 cups beef broth

salt and pepper

SAUTÉED VEAL CHOPS WITH WILD RAMPS

Serves 4

While many people in New England are familiar with wild fiddlehead ferns, which emerge in early spring, wild ramps are less well known. Ramps are a wild onion, sort of a cross between scallions and baby leeks, with a long slender leaf on top, and a thin white root. Surprisingly, the greens are much more strongly flavored than the white root. They are quite strong eaten raw, but when cooked their flavor is not nearly as sharp. The greens can be minced liked scallions, or the whole ramp, roughly the size of a scallion, can be braised. Gather wild ramps yourself in wet areas, or purchase them in gourmet markets, but the season is brief, so eat them while you can. Scallions may be used instead if ramps are not available, although their flavor is milder.

1. Preheat oven to 400°

2. In a large skillet, heat a little olive oil, and after seasoning the chops with salt and pepper, add them to the pan. Let brown well on one side, for about 3 minutes, add the garlic and ramps, and brown for 3 minutes on the other side.

3. Place the skillet in the oven for about 5 minutes, and then remove the skillet from the oven.

4. On top of the stove, add the Madeira or port to the pan, and let reduce by about half. Then add the veal stock and simmer until the liquid reduces by about half.

5. Remove the chops from the skillet, place the braised ramps on top and pour the remaining sauce over the chops. Serve immediately, with mashed potatoes.

4 loin veal chops,
12 ounces each

olive oil

½ teaspoon
minced garlic

2 bunches ramps

1 cup Madeira or port

2 cups veal stock

salt and pepper

CHEF'S ESSAYS

Wrestling with Bones

Many customers and home cooks, and others interested in food, sometimes ask or wonder what it is like to be a professional chef. People frequently ask me how I know how much food to order. Or after visiting the café on a busy night, and peeking into the partially open kitchen, wonder how it is possible to serve so many people such different menu items simultaneously. My usual response is: "The same way you get to Carnegie Hall." Aside from the volume of food prepared, perhaps the biggest difference between a Western or European-style professional restaurant kitchen and a home kitchen is the making and use of stock.

It is how most of my days begin and end—wrestling with bones. Making stock, particularly dark meat stock, requires a lot of time, space and strength. One of the first things I do after entering the restaurant is to haul a fifty-pound box of beef or veal bones out of the walk-in refrigerator and place them in a large roasting pan that is about eight square feet, and roast them for about two and a half hours. This monopolizes an oven for quite a bit of time. In a busy restaurant, in which a lot of baking is done, and use of the oven is required for other cooking, this is best done in the morning, before dinner service begins.

After the bones are well browned, but not burned, they are removed from the oven and transferred to large stock-pots. Any serious professional kitchen has at least one large stockpot that can accommodate about ten or more gallons of liquid. In addition to the bones, I add mirepoix, the French word for the holy trinity of carrots, onion and celery. Thyme, bay leaves and peppercorns are also essential ingredients. In addition to the roasting, which darkens the color of the stock, what also makes stock brown is the addition of tomato paste, which also thickens the resulting stock.

This is not for the faint of heart, or anyone squeamish about handling a large pile of knees, ankles and femurs. While many people think that the valuable part of an animal is the flesh, and that the bones are waste, chefs know and value bones for the flavor they impart to food, and the stock, which is prepared from their bones. It may seem counterintuitive, but bone, and specifically marrow, makes far more flavorful stock than the meat itself. The meat is best roasted, grilled or sautéed and eaten; the bones slowly simmered to make stock for soups or sauces.

These large pots of bones require simmering at low temperatures for a long time, and because of the amount of time required, and the space they occupy on the stove, they cannot be simmered during the day, or while the café is serving dinner. So the large pots are placed in the walk-in refrigerator until the end of the evening. Large volumes of liquid are necessary, because by the time the stock is slowly cooked and strained, the final result will yield a much smaller volume.

After a busy night serving dinner, and then cleaning up the kitchen one of the last tasks is to retrieve the stock-pots, which when loaded with bones weigh about thirty-five pounds each, from the walk-in refrigerator, and place them on the stove and fill them up with cold water. The stock must be brought to a low simmer, and then the flame turned down very low, so the liquid barely bubbles. The stock simmers slowly overnight, for about twelve hours. It is essential that the flame be adjusted perfectly; too low, and the stock doesn't cook; too high, and it will boil over during the night, risking fire, or burn the bottom of the pot, resulting in a burned and acrid flavor.

Upon opening the door and entering the café in the morning the first sensation that greets me is the fragrant bouquet of simmering stock, unmistakable anywhere.

The next step in making stock is to remove the bones from the liquid and discard them. They have imparted their entire flavor to the liquid, and at this point have no further value—except to large dogs. Well-prepared stock contains virtually no fat. This is because any fat or grease rises to the surface, which is skimmed off and removed. The old expression that scum rises to the top of a boiling pot is literally true, and the next step in preparing stock is to do just that. Bring the liquid to a boil to skim off any impurities, as well as to reduce and concentrate the flavor.

Depending on the intended uses, the stock is further cooked to reduce the volume, which thickens the liquid. As water boils off and evaporates, the stock becomes thicker and more concentrated. The French term is demi-glacé, literally half-stock, meaning that the volume of liquid is reduced by half. This is what most restaurants, including Castle Street Café, make and use. What started out as ten gallons of thin liquid ends up turning into five gallons of rich, highly concentrated flavor. The last and final step in the process is to pass the liquid through a fine, wire mesh strainer, which removes any solids from the stock, and ensures a fine-textured, smooth liquid.

From start to finish the process takes somewhere between twenty-four and thirty-six hours. It is a lot of work, and almost no home cooks, no matter how accomplished, do this. And it is one of the defining differences between even the most lovingly prepared home food and professionally cooked restaurant food.

If you want to make an omelet, you have to crack a few

eggs. Similarly, if you want to prepare some of the classics of European cuisine, like coq au vin, osso bucco, cassoulet, many other braised meats and soups, or complex sauces with wild mushrooms or Madeira, you need to make stock. There is simply no comparison between the instant or canned bouillon available in stores and real homemade stock. And that involves a lot of wrestling with bones.

In Praise of Braising

In the depths of winter we are drawn to the hearth and to the warmth of the kitchen, and to eating a heartier cuisine. An enormous percentage of our caloric intake is devoted to maintaining body temperature, so it's only natural that we require more fuel in the winter. This is the time of year for slow food, and there is no better example of that than slowly cooked braised food. Some of the classic dishes of European cuisine are based on braising, including coq au vin, osso bucco, cassoulet and beef burgundy.

As a general proposition, there are really only two speeds at which food is cooked. Grilling and sautéing are fast techniques, and braising and baking are slow methods. Braising is the cooking of food either partially or totally immersed in liquid, which can be stock, wine, or water, or some combination of these. Braising is an effective method of rendering tougher cuts of meat more tender, as muscle requires long slow cooking. These cuts of meat, like shoulder or shanks, are the less expensive parts of the animal, as opposed to the more premium loin. This is peasant food, and the opposite of prettily arranged plates of minimalist nouvelle cuisine. But when it's freezing outside, a pot roast is a lot more appealing than an artful arrangement of julienne snow peas.

It always helps to use stock when braising, but if that is not available, water my be substituted, though the resulting sauce will not be as rich or full-flavored. However, in the process of simmering meat slowly in liquid, you almost create your own stock. If the resulting sauce is too thin, it can always be thickened with flour or cornstarch, or better yet, reduced over heat to intensify and concentrate the flavor. The addition of a little tomato paste to beef dishes cooked in water will thicken the sauce and add intensity to the flavor. Wine also tenderizes muscle, and the classic preparations of coq au vin or beef burgundy rely heavily on the richness of the wine to flavor the meat and sauce.

A heavy-bottomed casserole is an ideal vessel for braising, and a secure lid is essential. The whole idea is to keep the liquid in, and if you attempt to cook something in liquid for a long time inside the oven without a lid, by the end of the process, most of the liquid will have evaporated. Braising is a forgiving cooking technique, because unlike a roast, which can become overcooked and dry, there is little risk of this when braising. While it's true that something cooked too long when braised may tend to fall apart, it will still be tender and delicious. A stewed chicken is supposed to almost fall off the bone.

In my first professional cooking job in New York many years ago, the restaurateur I worked for had one question he always asked upon hearing about a new dish I had prepared: "Is it juicy?" If it had been braised, the answer was surely yes.

Food and Art

The combination of a visit to the Impressionist exhibit at the Clark Museum and the planning of a new art opening at Castle Street Café of food paintings by Ellen Kaiden brought to the fore again the old chestnut of whether or not food is art.

Clearly people are attracted to eating some foods because they are visual and attractively presented. One of the things that distinguishes good restaurants is the skill of the chef in presenting food, as well as the ambience that designer china and place settings lend to a meal. Even a modestly skilled home cook has some sense of how to prepare and serve food so as to not have it resemble cafeteria fare. How many of us have remarked upon being served an attractive dish that it is so beautiful it seems a shame to eat it?

Nonetheless, I have always believed that the first priority of food is that it must taste good, and if in the course of preparing a dish I am forced to choose between something that might make the dish taste better as opposed to look attractive, I am always prepared to choose the former. While it is true we see food before we taste it, the main thing we do with food is eat it, not stare at it.

One of the excesses of nouvelle cuisine that we suffered through a decade or two ago was the preoccupation with arranging and fussing with food to the point where chefs were more concerned with presentation than with taste. In an effort to distinguish itself from the sometimes heavier French classics served by maître d's tableside in the dining room, a newer generation of chefs insisted on complete control of the presentation of a dish by plating everything in the kitchen, as opposed to tableside. One result of this was sometimes food that had been fussed with to the point where it was no longer hot, as well as the rightfully maligned minimalist presentations, which while spare and beautiful, contained little to actually eat.

Years ago I worked for a very successful New York City restaurateur who upon looking at a classic beef dish remarked: "This dish needs some red in it," without regard for how the addition of red peppers or tomatoes would affect the taste or integrity of the dish. As if cooking were like coloring by numbers.

Those with a passion for art should get some pastels, oils, or water colors, and like Cézanne, create their still lifes on canvas. But when cooking in the kitchen, let your tongue be your guide.

Ode to Carbohydrates

At the dawn of a new century many Americans are on guard against attack from what they regard as one of their most virulent enemies. No, I'm not referring to international terrorists, but rather those evil carbohydrates lurking around at every meal, and trying to infiltrate their bodies. We live in a culture preoccupied with food fads, and the latest and perhaps most widespread is the Atkins regime of eliminating carbs from our diet. By their very nature and definition, fads come and go. We have seen a variety come in and out of fashion, including low-fat and raw food and vegetarian, but the fear of carbohydrates has become widespread in our culture.

The data is controversial and by no means conclusive, but it is clear that many people manage to lose significant amounts of weight by vastly reducing the carbohydrates in their diet. Whether the substitution of and reliance on increased amounts of animal fat, which is one feature of the Atkins regime, is a healthy alternative, is another question. I do not pretend to be a medical doctor, and the implications of these radical swings in diet may not be clear for some time, and are best left to nutritionists and cardiologists. That we are a culture significantly overweight is undeniable.

Nonetheless there is something profoundly disturbing about the whole notion that basic food groups are "the enemy." So many people have adopted a kind of cold war mentality to their eating habits, with the food world being divided between good and evil foods. For millennia homo sapiens have relied on a variety of grains and carbohydrates as the foundation of their diet, and their elimination from our diet really represents a fundamental shift in the way we eat.

From the dawn of time the cultivation of wheat and rice has been central to human activity. Far more than a category of food, they have served to define entire cultures. Wheat has been the staff of life, and our daily bread, and to completely eliminate it from our diet is indeed a great loss. The breaking of and sharing of bread is a key element in most Western religious traditions, and one we ought not to abandon lightly.

The real tragedy is that in most parts of this country it is virtually impossible today to buy anything remotely resembling "real" bread. The bleached and highly refined air breads that line the shelves of most supermarkets is so far removed from whole grain and naturally leavened breads as to require a different name. In the Berkshires we are fortunate to have a variety of local and regional artisan breadmakers whose products are widely available in natural foods markets and co-ops, but that is far less true in most of the rest of the country.

If reducing or eliminating carbohydrates is a radical notion in the West, it is even more so in Asia. The overwhelming majority of the world are rice eaters, and the elimination of this foundation from their diet would be tantamount to starvation. Obesity is not a widespread problem in most of the rice-eating cultures of the world, where tiny amounts of protein are consumed, compared to developed Western countries. Nor do the rice-eating cultures of the world suffer from heightened cholesterol and heart disease the way that Western countries do. In many developing and impoverished countries there is simply no alternative to eating rice. The capacity to freely change and adjust diets is a luxury available to only a small percent of those of us in the wealthy developed countries.

It is counterintuitive, but for some reason extreme measures appeal to many of us more than moderate ones. A diversified diet that includes moderate quantities of less highly refined carbohydrates, like whole grain breads and rice, somehow seems like a more difficult diet to follow than the extreme measures that almost completely eliminate consumption of carbohydrates. As it is in the investment world, balance and diversity are the foundation of a healthy diet, and the pursuit of extreme measures is unsustainable and unhealthy in the long run.

It Takes a Team

Sportscasters frequently comment that baseball, basketball and football are team sports, which rely on the skills and talents of all the team members to win games, especially at the highest level. One star player does not a team make. Home run legends and ace pitchers are great to have on a team, but only if they play with the support of the other teammates.

A restaurant operates as a team as well, with almost as many players as a pro sports team, and cooperation and mutual understanding and support are essential if it is to operate properly. To begin with, even a modest size restaurant has many cooks in the kitchen, each of whom has specific tasks to perform, and who are each involved in preparation of different aspects of your dinner. Just because the restaurant has a renowned chef doesn't mean he oversees every dish that is served. Even in the best restaurants, many meals get served for which the chef has relied on cooks and subordinates to execute recipes. There are pastry chefs, salad chefs, and many others who have prepared parts of your meal, and the chef may not have been involved at all.

One of the oldest divides in restaurants is between those who work in the "front of the house," and those who work in the "back of the house," and it is true there is a difference between working as a waiter or as a cook. Rivalries and tempers can sometimes flare and this almost always results in a worse dining experience for the customer. Diners may have special requests that require accommodation and the attention of cooks, and their cooperation is required to provide a good meal. Waiters sometimes forget to place a diners order in the kitchen, and cooks have been known to forget an order, or seriously overcook it. They must work together to overcome errors and mistakes, regardless of who made them. Out in the dining room, there is just a diner who wants his steak cooked right. I have witnessed traditional French chefs berate a waiter to the point of tears, and then send him out into the dining room. A wait staff that is terrorized in the kitchen by a prima donna chef, or feels reluctant to ask for special orders to satisfy particular customers, can't possibly provide good service.

Hosts and maître d's have their own special role to play, greeting old customers as they enter, knowing people's name and favorite table, and how they like their drink. The late James Beard, when asked to name his favorite restaurant, was reported to have replied, "The place where they know me." Being known, and treated as a welcome guest, is possible only when staff turnover is low, and familiar staff recognize familiar diners.

The teamwork extends to the provisioning of the kitchen. A good restaurant often has a long and close relationship with small farmers and specialty suppliers. Small farmers and chefs work together to inform and support each other, to provide the quality ingredients essential for making good food. The trust and rapport is an outgrowth of years of working together toward the same goal.

The least heralded members of the team, whose work is crucial to the operation of the team, are those who do the dish and pot washing, and constant clean up. It is a thankless and unglamorous task, and too often not acknowledged. There is nothing like a dishwasher calling in sick to make you realize how essential their role is.

So while it's fun to dine at restaurants run by celebrity chefs, it takes a team to make a great meal, and many of those team players never get the recognition they deserve.

Working The Magic

There is an old expression used by vaudeville veterans and theatre professionals to describe their skills and achievements in pulling off a successful evening of entertainment. "Working the Magic" refers to all the hard work done by producers, directors and performers that culminates in a dazzling evening of live performance. When the curtain goes up, and the lights go down, few in the audience are aware of all the hard work executed beforehand. Like a figure skater, high wire performer, or ballerina twirling on one foot, it's got to look effortless. No one in the audience wants to see the performers sweating and breathing heavily. When the tuxedoed magician reaches into the top hat, there can't be any doubt about the rabbit being inside.

There are many people in a wide range of fields who are supremely skilled at making the impossible seem effortless. Professional athletes whose presence dominates a clutch game; surgeons who perform life-saving operations, and teachers who manage to impart knowledge and inspiration to their young charges all know what working the magic means and is.

In many ways running a restaurant is a performance art that has a lot in common with a Broadway show. Every night the doors open, the audience fills the seats, and the show goes on. The Berkshires, which outside of New York City or Los Angeles is perhaps America's premier cultural destination, with world class dance, theatre and music, is also home to an unusually high number of high quality, chef- owned restaurants, which serve distinctive cuisine, made from locally raised ingredients. This is not a coincidence.

An evening at Tanglewood, Jacob's Pillow, or the Mahaiwe Theatre frequently begins with a dinner preceding the show, and that is where the evening's entertainment starts. Diners need and want to know that they are going to have a delicious meal served in a timely fashion in order to get to the evening performance, and it is the restaurant's duty to provide that.

Diners have their own responsibilities. These include showing up on time for a reservation, letting servers know that they are going to theatre, and allowing themselves enough time to dine in a relaxed manner. When both diners and restaurants honor their respective obligations, everyone has a successful and enjoyable evening. Like many things in life, it takes two to tango.

No one bats a thousand. Great orchestras occasionally play out of tune; veteran actors sometimes forget lines; good restaurants overcook steak and fish and make diners wait for tables. But the truly good performers don't screw up often. As in the way to get to Carnegie Hall, with enough practice, one gets skilled at working the magic.

Tradition and Innovation

When an orchestra like the Boston Symphony programs their season at Tanglewood, you can be sure to find familiar and traditional favorites, combined with new and cutting edge experimental works. The trick is to program the classics of the repertoire with new works by contemporary composers in a balanced way. While many listeners would be happy to limit their listening to Beethoven and Mozart and other musical war horses, the failure to include newer works risks rendering the programming stodgy and tired.

Chefs face a similar consideration when creating and devising menus. No one wants to eat the same food over and over again, yet there is no denying the allure of comfort foods. In the past generation there has been an enormous revolution in how we eat, and the challenge to balance tradition and innovation is very much an issue today.

Only a little over a generation ago "serious food" in this

country meant French cuisine, and one had to know how to prepare and execute the well-defined classics of the cuisine. For chefs of a certain generation, the cookbook they relied on was called *The Repertoire of the Cuisine*, which defined those French classics, like Beef Wellington, grilled Dover sole, and all the variations on Hollandaise sauce. If you add orange zest to the sauce, it's called sauce Maltaise, and if tarragon is added it is known as Béarnaise. Cooking was like the short program in olympic skating; there were defined standards that one had to perform, and chefs were judged not on creativity, but on how well they executed predetermined exercises.

It was against this highly codified tradition that a younger generation of chefs rebelled in the early sixties, as part of the larger social revolution that was sweeping the world. Chefs wanted the freedom to create dishes in their own style, and they did. While earlier generations of French chefs relied almost exclusively on their own cultural heritage and were scarcely even aware of or interested in other national cuisines, in the sixties and seventies these chefs began to embrace elements of Asian, American, and other European cuisines in their cooking.

Today the globalization of cooking techniques has become so pervasive that it's hard to find restaurants and chefs that haven't embraced at least some aspects of other national cuisines. French restaurants serve pasta, Japanese restaurants make rolls with avocados, and American restaurants use lemongrass. Today it's hard to find a restaurant that serves the kind of old-fashioned French cuisine that includes a lot of Hollandaise-based sauces.

To be sure, there were and still are excesses in the effort to create new dishes. In the eighties I worked in a Manhattan restaurant that had as one of its signature dishes Tomato Orange Soup. Tomato goes well with lemon, and it's only a short stretch to change the lemon to orange. The proprietor was intrigued with citrus, and he was interested in creating other soups with a citrus theme. In a menu brainstorming session, I made what I thought was the out-rageously ridiculous and tongue in cheek suggestion of trying broccoli-grapefruit soup. He thought that was a brilliant idea, and urged me to make it the following day. Rest assured it tasted as awful as it sounds.

The pressure to devise new dishes often pushes chefs into creating recipes best left uneaten. I recently ate in one of New York's most highly rated restaurants, and dessert was a warm chocolate cake served with caramelized fennel and fennel ice cream.

The chocolate cake was good, and while I like fennel in salads, or with chicken or fish, it makes a poor combination with chocolate. It's true that the pairing was innovative, but there is a good reason few others have tried it. Plain old vanilla ice cream would have tasted so much better, but it wouldn't have been cutting edge.

Two very different trends are prominent in the food world today. Inspired in part by pioneering chefs like Alice Waters, who made the search for well-grown ingredients a primary concern, the quest for organic and locally grown ingredients continues to be a focus for many chefs, particularly here in the Berkshires. Menu ideas are inspired by the availability of high quality local ingredients, which unite chefs and their menus with local farmers.

At what is perhaps the opposite end of the spectrum, another trend is the attempt to use cutting edge cooking techniques to manipulate food in ways that have not been done before. This interest in using new cooking techniques is most closely associated with the Spanish chef Ferran Adria, of the restaurant El Bulli in northern Spain.

His restaurant is the mecca for some young chefs today who are interested in learning how to create the signature foams, powders, and gelatins for which Adria is known. He has mentored and trained a new generation of young Spanish chefs, and for the first time in recent history, a chef from Spain has become perhaps the most renowned chef in the world. El Bulli is only open six months a year, and only serves fifty dinners a night, and I have not had the opportunity to dine there. During the other six months a year, Adria works in an experimental kitchen using techniques like freezing and pulverizing ingredients to create new dishes. One of his signature dishes is an asparagus pasta that he creates by making a gelatin sheet out of cooked asparagus, and cutting it into thin strips like fettuccine, which is served cool. We've come a long way from pasta with red sauce.

Chef Adria is fascinated with using high-tech cooking techniques to alter our concept of food, and in using new techniques to change the way food is prepared. While I am curious to eat there, much of the inspiration for his food strikes me as strained and in some fundamental way divorced from nature.

In the same way that most humans are naturally attracted to harmony and melody, and find it difficult to comprehend the dissonance and atonal quality of much contemporary avant garde classical music, we are also naturally attracted to the comfort food we grew up with. When Stravinsky's *Rite of Spring* was first performed, it caused outrage, but today it is part of the standard repertoire, and is almost mainstream compared to contemporary compositions. Perhaps in another generation or two, Chef Adria's foams and gelatins will become just as accepted. Nevertheless, there will always be a place for braised chicken on restaurant menus, as there will be for Mozart in orchestral programs. The trick is to balance tradition with innovation.

Farming Fish

The educated eating public has had a lot of information to contend with the over the past few years, as various concerns about the healthfulness of the American diet, and the manner in which food is produced in this country have become front page news. Warnings about the dangers of eating meat and cholesterol have perhaps been displaced lately by fear of carbohydrates, and concerns about chemical additives and fast food have received a lot of attention, but until very recently one food item has enjoyed the status of being almost universally regarded as being part of a healthy diet—fresh fish.

Consumption of fresh fish has boomed in this country in recent years, as those trying to moderate their intake of red meat have switched to eating more fish, and even those on Atkins-type diets rely on fish as an important part of their meals. The recent widespread popularity of sushi in this country is just one measure of the change in American eating habits.

Alas, even this refuge from the pervasive anxiety about the safety and healthfulness of our diet has been under assault lately, as information about the environmental harm caused by modern practices of fish farming have received prominent attention in *The New York Times* and other publications. The sad fact is that the plummeting population of wild fish swimming freely in the ocean has led to an increasing reliance on aquaculture to produce the fish we eat. When commercial aquaculture was first introduced about twenty years ago in Norway and Canada, it was hailed by chefs and consumers as a boon to fish consumption, and indeed the supply and price has been remarkable. However, years later, the environmental issues are causing concerns.

The impetus for developing commercial aquaculture is clear: there are fewer and fewer fish left in the oceans. In just the last generation, fishing stocks have been reduced by giant industrial fishing fleets, which have left the size and number of fisheries diminished. Some species, like Chilean sea bass, have gone from being commercially negligible and not widely eaten to an endangered species in scarcely one generation. The once fertile Chesapeake and Cape Cod bays, renowned for their shellfish, are experiencing diminished harvests. Other areas, like our own Housatonic and Hudson, are off-limits because of PCB and other pollution. Global warming and the damming of rivers have also taken their toll. As a result, the vast majority of the salmon and shrimp we now eat are produced on commercial aquaculture farms, rather than caught swimming wild. The once wild Atlantic salmon, found throughout the rivers of New England, is officially an endangered species.

Among the concerns about commercial aquaculture are the threat to wild fish stocks from escaped farmed fish, and the contamination of the ocean from the concentration of vast fish populations in a small area. Just as heirloom plant growers strive to protect the biological diversity and heritage of the plant world as an alternative to crop monoculture, the same is true of those trying to protect it in the fish world. And just as independent farmers are widely being replaced by a handful of multinational corporations that control vast quantities of the world's food supply, independent fisherman are being replaced by a few multinational corporations that control most of the aquaculture.

All is not grim. As a result of stringent regulation, the once endangered striped bass has had a resurgence, and is more widely available now. For a few weeks of summer, these majestic fish are caught in the wild, and are available in fish markets. For those too accustomed to eating their farmed brethren, the experience of eating a fish caught wild in the ocean is without comparison.

Foliage Cuisine

It's not just the leaves that turn color as the autumn progresses in New England; some of the traditional fall foods have the same autumn colors. The squashes, pumpkins and gourds reflect the colors of the changing leaves, and fall cuisine is more substantial than summer fare.

The number of winter or hard squashes available at local farm stands is almost as varied as the heirloom tomatoes of summer. In addition to the familiar butternut and acorn squashes, there are hubbard, buttercup, red curry, delicato, Long Island cheese pumpkins, kabocha, spaghetti, and many others as well. The names themselves are mesmerizing. While many people think that this great variety of squashes is mostly for decorative purposes, they make for great eating. These are usually priced so inexpensively that you can't afford not to eat them.

Butternut is my favorite for making soup, because they peel so easily and the shape lends themselves to peeling and dicing. Acorns are probably most commonly baked and glazed, but they are also great for stuffing and baking. There are many who believe that a pumpkin pie isn't the real thing unless it's made with fresh pumpkin; the canned variety is usually thicker and less watery, but I confess I can't tell the difference once all the spices and sugar are added.

Kale is another of those autumn vegetables more frequently used for decoration than eating, but those who have never tried it don't know what they are missing. I am in agreement with those south of the Mason-Dixon who believe that the hearty greens like kale and mustard greens go best with a liberal quantity of bacon or salt pork, which have a natural affinity with these greens.

While many people assume that cooking with apples means dessert like apple pie and crisp, cooked apples make a great accompaniment for pork and duck, as well as scallops and salmon. Firm tart apples like Granny Smiths are good for cooking, while softer apples like Macintosh are not well suited for cooking. Pears can be substituted in the same dishes just as well. The same pear that is too hard to eat when just purchased at the market will be rendered soft and juicy after a little braising in liquid. The natural sweetness of the fruit goes well with these dishes, as well as sauces made from hard cider. There are several hard ciders made in the Berkshires, which go well with food cooked with fruit.

It's a shame that many people only eat cranberries as part of a Thanksgiving dinner, because they are too delicious to eat only so rarely. It's true that they require a lot of sugar to be palatable to most, but they also go well with pork, duck, or game. Cranberries make a delicious and colorful sorbet, and can be used in cobblers and crisps, either alone or combined with apples. Dried cranberries can be used like raisins, either in baked goods, or in sauces.

For those entertaining, you can still decorate your table with these colorful autumn vegetables, but just remember that they are delicious to eat as well.

Giving the Gift of Food

The month of December is a time of year many of us do a lot of gift giving, but many people approach the shopping season with dread and apprehension over another trip to the mall. The thought of fighting crowds and slogging through snow-covered parking lots can certainly deter all but the most intrepid shoppers.

If you want to give a gift that is truly personal and allows you to express yourself creatively, there's no better gift than the gift of food. There are very few people who don't appreciate the gift of homemade cookies or candies, or preserves made from fruit from your garden. The gift of food demonstrates that you cared enough to spend time in the kitchen actually preparing food, rather than merely buying something.

Sweets, baked goods and desserts are the obvious starting off point. One way to satisfy a lot of different people is to buy decorative metal tins and bake a variety of different kinds of cookies. An assortment of chocolate, sugar, butter and lace cookies makes a delicious gift. In order to eliminate the last minute crunch, start early and freeze some of the cookies, and assemble the tins just before the holidays. Quick breads like banana bread or zucchini bread also make great gifts, and can be wrapped attractively.

Traditionalists and Anglophiles should start early with the preparations of their steamed puddings and plum cakes, in order for the liquor in those to be properly absorbed. Chocolate truffles require refrigeration, but they too are simple to make and will make a big hit with your favorite chocoholics.

Gifts don't have to be limited to dessert. Homemade vinegar can be made by steeping herbs or fruit in white vinegar to make tarragon or raspberry vinegar. Antique bottles can be stuffed with dried chili peppers and filled with olive oil to make a zesty spiced oil.

If you are limited in time and kitchen skills, you can always break down and buy some gourmet ingredients for those people you know who like to cook. A tin of saffron or caviar, a well-aged bottle of balsamic vinegar, or a prestigious Château from a good vintage will surely be appreciated. But the extra effort involved in preparing something yourself will hopefully provide as much satisfaction for the giver as for the recipient.

Fiddleheads, Shad Roe, & Soft Shells

In the contemporary global economy we now take for granted that we can walk into a modern supermarket or specialty grocery and buy just about any ingredient any time of year. Ingredients that were once highly seasonal food items are now increasingly available most of the year. There is asparagus from South America in the dead of winter, and blueberries from New Zealand at a time of year when New Englanders would never think of making a pie. It's only been a few generations since people survived on the turnips and carrots in their root cellars until the harvest of their next garden.

Nonetheless there are still some cycles of nature that remain untampered with, and which remind us of the ebb and flow of the seasons. In spring, three of nature's most marvelous creations begin their natural cycle, and it behooves us to take advantage of their brief availability.

For a few short weeks of early spring, fiddlehead ferns are available, and few edible plants have such a short cycle. They are only edible in their curled-up stage, and it's just a matter of days between their first appearance above the ground and the time when they are fully mature and no longer edible. Soak them in cold water to remove any fuzz or hair-like material. They are best briefly sautéed, and while they have a very mild flavor, they are pleasantly crisp.

When the weather turns a little warm the great migration of the shad begins to the rivers of New England. The Hudson and Connecticut rivers are two of the main sources of shad, and for most people it is the roe more than the flesh that is prized. Shad roe is one of those foods like sweetbreads or caviar; you either like it or you don't, and there isn't much middle ground. The roe is contained in a large sac surrounded by a thin membrane, which holds the thousands of tiny fish eggs together. The trick is to handle the sac very carefully, and to sauté it or bake it for about five minutes, all the way handling it very gingerly. The season only lasts for a few weeks, so you must enjoy them while you can. Traditional New England recipes, which are a legacy of the Portuguese settlers, frequently combine the shad roe with bacon and onions.

By the end of May the first of the season's soft-shell crabs are available, and a mild winter will likely mean an a slightly earlier season. As the blue crab from the Chesapeake Bay area grow and molt their shell, for a few brief hours their outer shell is soft, and it is then that they are harvested. They are highly prized by fish lovers during their soft shell stage, and you'll have to be prepared to shell out a high price for them, but the reward is worth it, and the season brief. A coating of flour helps make them even crisper, and a squeeze of lemon and some minced garlic are all you need.

Even with the abundance of food available to us in our local markets, these seasonal specialties are a treat, because they are only available for a short time, and a reminder of the earth's natural cycle, with which we have become all too out of touch.

Marinating, and The Art of the Grill

Memorial Day marks the beginning of the official grilling season, and there are a couple of keys to successful grilling. Many people will be taking their grill out of the garage or barn for the first time since last season, and the first thing to do is to make sure the wire grates are clean and don't have the well-charred remains of last year's dinner still clinging to the grill. A stiff wire brush is essential for maintaining a clean grill, and should be used to clean the grill after every use.

Perhaps the most important consideration is the kind of fuel used in your grill. Gas is certainly the easiest, and those with gas grills don't face any decision at all. But for all those who are accustomed to buying the traditional charcoal briquettes, there is another choice. While they are certainly less expensive, the standard charcoal briquettes, which require lighter fluid to start them, are full of petroleum products, and have a distinct chemical smell. It is possible to buy natural hardwood charcoal, which are irregularly shaped chunks of real charcoal. This is true natural charcoal, which burns considerably hotter and faster than the standard commercial variety. It is more expensive, but well worth the difference. And for those who have trimmed their fruit trees earlier in the year and have dried apple or other hardwood to burn, don't hesitate to burn this in your grill.

It's much easier to cook food that is of uniform thickness, which avoids burning the outside while the inside remains undercooked. It's a lot easier to cook breast of chicken then whole chicken pieces. A plastic misting bottle filled with vegetable oil is very useful in spraying the grill surface with a fine mist of oil, which helps prevent food from sticking to the grill. The flame will flare up for a brief moment when the oil is first sprayed on the grill, but after the initial flame subsides the grill will be well-lubricated. In addition, this will help you make crosshatch grill marks, which are one of the hallmarks of grilled food. Place the item to be cooked on the grill for about half the time you want it cooked on the first side, and then use a spatula or pair of tongs to rotate the food ninety degrees, and finish cooking on the first side. When you turn it over, it should have the classic crosshatch grill marks.

And last, but certainly not least, is the subject of marinades. It's one of the givens of summer entertaining in the country that dinner will be cooked outdoors, and perhaps eaten there as well. With a little bit of effort, you can transform plain grilled food into something much more flavorful, by just marinating the food for a few hours. It doesn't take a lot of time to prepare a marinade, and only takes a few hours of contact for the flavors to seep in, although overnight will result in a stronger, deeper flavor.

Two of the basic ingredients are acid and herbs. Acid usually takes the form of lemon juice or vinegar, which tenderizes tough muscles, making food soften, therefore easier to eat. As with vinaigrette, the proportions are generally about 3-1 oil to vinegar. For herbs to have any effect, they must be fresh, because the dried flakes stored in the small bottles in your kitchen cabinet will add very little flavor to anything. Those who have been industrious enough to plant their own herb garden need only to snip some fresh tarragon, chives, or sage leaf to add a powerful seasoning to any dish. Use your own taste to add whatever fresh herbs are your favorite.

Marinades need not be complicated. One of the most time honored is the basic Asian marinade using soy sauce, ginger, scallions and garlic. Some prefer the addition of sugar to this, and sesame oil, rice wine vinegar and sherry all may be added. Equally basic is a marinade made from fresh-squeezed lemon juice and grated lemon zest with the addition of olive oil and garlic. Grilled shrimp or scallops, as well as poultry, are delicious with this marinade. If you prefer something a little sweeter, substitute oranges for the lemons. The citrus still works, but the result is not quite so acidic.

Those seeking a more assertive marinade may want to try one based on balsamic vinegar, with olive oil, garlic, and fresh tarragon or rosemary. The balsamic vinegar darkens whatever is being marinated, but it's particularly good with beef or lamb. Tamarind has an even stronger flavor. Tamarind paste is made from tamarind seeds, and is characteristic of Indian as well as South American cuisine. Tamarind paste is quite bitter and requires considerable sweetening, but combined with ginger it makes a very distinctive seasoning. Another partially prepared sauce that can be the basis of an Asian marinade is hoisin sauce. Hoisin sauce is made from fermented soy beans, which are sweetened, and with the addition of ginger and orange juice, it makes a sweeter variation on the basic Asian soy-based marinade.

Whatever marinade you use, feel free to brush it liberally on whatever you have grilled for even more flavor. But be careful to avoid putting on any liquid that had uncooked meat or fish in it without fully cooking it first. And when the food is finished cooking, a garnish of snipped chives or a chiffonade of basil directly from the herb garden completes your meal.

Blueberries and Tomatoes

The cuisine of summer can perhaps be summed up in two of my favorite ingredients: blueberries and tomatoes. Not that I suggest combining these two in any one dish. It is when these two ingredients are ripe and available in local farm stands that you know it's summer.

It's true that blueberries are available earlier in the season from areas south of here, but it is usually in July or August that they are at the peak of their season in New England. And while you can buy berries at both farm stands and supermarkets, there is nothing like picking them yourself, then going home and making your own pie. Blueberries are abundant in Berkshire County and the surrounding Taconic Hills, and there is scarcely a state park in the area that doesn't have some growing. There are also a number of pick-your-own farms throughout the area. One of the most scenic is atop Mt. Washington near Bash Bish Falls, which makes a great afternoon outing of berry picking and waterfall viewing.

Pies, cobblers, pancakes and muffins are just some of the potential uses for blueberries, but they can also be enjoyed more simply with a little grated lemon and splash of Gran Marnier. There is some debate about whether blueberry pie is better enjoyed warm or chilled, but I have always believed that a warm pie facilitates the melting of vanilla ice cream, which is a virtue. But it is a crime to place ice cream on top of a flaky crust, which will render it soggy.

The explosion in the varieties of tomatoes available in the marketplace is extraordinary. There are literally hundreds of varieties of heirloom tomatoes being cultivated locally, spanning the color range from deep red to purple and almost black, as well as green, yellow, and orange. You simply can't get tomatoes like this in January at any price, and it almost seems sinful to eat anything else when jewels like these have such a fleeting season. Nothing is more appropriate to summer entertaining than a display of a wide variety of sizes and colors of tomatoes drizzled with a little olive oil, either with or without some fresh mozzarella.

Don't be put off by cracked, bruised, or slightly damaged tomatoes, because these are often the most tasty, and frequently sold at a discount. They are perfect for making gazpacho, sauces, or just peeling and chopping and tossing in pasta salad. If you aren't industrious enough to make and can your own sauce, you can dry and temporarily preserve your own tomatoes by cutting them in half, drizzling them with a little olive oil, and drying them at a very low temperature, such as 125° or 150°, in a convection oven. The result will not be as dry as a commercially dried tomato, but much of the water will evaporate, yielding a chewy dense texture.

Hyacinth Therapy

The early spring is a tough time in the Berkshires. If we've had any snow at all, it's starting to melt. The ski season is over, but it's too muddy to go hiking, and too chilly to go swimming. The big cultural organizations have yet to open for the year, fewer second-home owners spend time here, and even locals often choose this time to get away on vacation. In the culinary world, the farmers' markets are closed, and the new year's supply of fresh goat cheese will not be available for some time. Local greenhouse farmers, who often manage to stay in business through the holiday season, are working on the next year's plantings, and not harvesting any fresh greens yet. It's true you can buy asparagus in the market, but it is not from around here, and those tiny anorexic spears from Peru and Chile are a poor substitute for the heartier domestic version. Though the days are getting longer instead of shorter, winter almost invariably and inexplicably takes its toll, and by March even the sturdiest among us are experiencing a certain amount of seasonal affective disorder, otherwise known as the winter blues.

Allow me to propose a cure: hyacinth therapy. For a few months in early spring the floral world is at its height. At least in my mind, or should I say nose, flowers reach their pinnacle in those wonderfully fragrant blossoms that sprout up in early spring, particularly hyacinths.

All flowers are pretty, but only some smell nice. Why bother with flowers that only look pretty, when there are flowers that also smell great? Roses also have a great smell, but they are expensive, and generally too fussed over. Smell is the most primal and intimate of senses, and influences us in ways we scarcely even understand. It seems strange and counterintuitive, but in the heat of summer, many if not most of the flowers that bloom have very little fragrance, compared to those that bloom earlier. In mid-summer we buy wild flowers from local farmers for use in the restaurant, and they are lovely. They just don't smell, and if you happen not to look their way, you may not even notice them.

There is fine line between taste and smell. It is sometimes hard to tell where the line begins, but it surely exists. While I enjoy the smell of flowers, I don't want to eat them. The nouvelle practice of serving edible flowers like nasturtiums seems too precious and pretentious. But scent is intricately connected to food and the stimulation and arousal of appetite. Some smells are irresistible, and unquestioningly gratifying, like that of bread baking, garlic sizzling, or chocolate melting. It is the aroma of food cooking that initially stimulates our appetites, and creates that delightful anticipation of a good meal. We can continue to take in the bouquet of food cooking, and it does not decrease our appetite. While appetizers on menus are supposed to whet our appetite, they usually do the opposite, because as soon as we eat, our appetite begins to decline. Perhaps the ultimate appetizers in restaurants ought to be strictly olfactory-courses we inhale, but don't actually eat.

There is a direct relationship between sensitivity to and enjoyment of smell, and appreciation of food, and these food scents might be the best way to tease our appetites before a meal. One way a good restaurant makes its quality known, before you ever eat even a morsel, is by the smell of good food wafting through the dining room. How many times have you been out to dinner and smelled something going by, or being served at the next table, and immediately wanted to order that dish?

In early spring, when the shad have yet to run, before the soft-shell crabs begin to molt, and half a year before we can harvest a real tomato, there are few things more uplifting then getting enough hyacinths so that their fragrance fills a room. The café has broad windowsills that catch a lot of early morning sun, and are great for plants. When it is hyacinth season, and the flowers are in bloom, it is an extraordinary sensation to open the door in the morning and be greeted by the smell of their bouquet.

At a time of year when there is so very little available in the way of local produce, thank goodness for hyacinths, which give us the strength to carry on until summer.

Food Memories

I recently catered a small party for a man in his late sixties celebrating a birthday, and while he was flexible about the menu selection and choice of entrée, the dessert had to be lemon meringue pie with a graham cracker crust. He was quite precise about the specifications and details. Why this dessert? Like Proust before him, this was his memory of birthday dinners as a child growing up, and a forkful reconnected him with his fond childhood memories. Birthdays are occasions on which food memories are particularly associated. As a child growing up, one of the perks of the birthday celebrant was being able to choose the birthday menu, not unlike a condemned man's last meal. While over the years my choice of entrée changed, dessert remained constant. I don't know the origin of the name, but the rich butter cake with cinnamon and walnuts, known around my family as He-man Cake, remains to this day one of my all-time favorites, and a requisite part of my birthday celebration. My father's birthday was unthinkable without a blueberry pie from the first of the season's berries.

We all have food memories that transport us and connect us to other times. As a chef I always issue a disclaimer that my rendition may not live up to cherished memories, and that my version will almost certainly never be as good as someone's mother.

Some food memories stand out because the first time we eat a certain food, it makes a lasting impression. I recall distinctly the first time I tasted great wine, which gave me some insight into why some people so highly value rare, old Bordeaux. As a young chef working in New York, I had some opportunity to taste wines in the restaurants in which I worked, and I was familiar with the names Lafite and Latour, though I had never tasted them. At the conclusion of a special wine tasting dinner featuring classified Bordeaux from some of the most renowned châteaux, I had the chance to sit down and taste 25-year-old fully mature wines, and it was a revelation. So this is why people are willing to pay a lot of money for great wine! This truly was different from the wine I had so far been exposed to.

Some food memories are just as vivid, if not as pleasant. On a trip to France, which featured eating at a variety of different restaurants of interest, I found myself in L'Ami Louis, one of the most heralded old bistros in Paris. They were famous for their version of tripe, which I had never before eaten. I figured if there were ever a place to try it, this was certainly it. This was one of the reasons I had come to France—to further my culinary education and explore new tastes. I had a slight, but only vague notion of what I had ordered. Suffice to say that what looked like a plate of rubber bands tasted much the same way.

Many food memories are associated with a particular place, and we have to travel to satisfy our yearnings. Lobster always tastes better at a favorite place along the Maine coast, the memory of gelato alone makes a trip to Tuscany worth it, and guavas and mangos eaten at home never taste like the ones eaten on a Caribbean beach.

Some food memories can be relived by recreating food that is so sufficiently close to the original that it brings forth that memory. However, other memories exist only as that, because recipes get lost, the transmission of family traditions gets interrupted, or despite trying, we are simply unable to replicate a favorite family dish in a manner that satisfies us. My grandmother's strudel was one of my favorite things to eat growing up, but she never gave the recipe to her daughter-in-law, my mother, and it remains only in my memory. Some say that Chesapeake oysters just don't taste as good now as they did many years ago, and perhaps the deterioration in the waters makes that all too true. As certain unusual varieties of heirloom produce become replaced by more commercially standard varieties, or even genetically altered ones, the memory of tomatoes and apples eaten in our youth may only exist as memories.

Then again, some food memories may be so embellished by time that they can never be lived up to in the present.

SAUCES

SAFFRON SAUCE
Serves 8

Saffron is the world's costliest spice, but a little bit goes a long way. A few threads of the dried herb are enough to impart to a dish its distinctive color and flavor. It is an essential ingredient in many classic dishes like risotto or bouillabaisse. The following recipe for saffron sauce can be used for either fish or poultry, and the pale yellow color of the sauce is particularly spring like. Served with a few spears of asparagus and a mince of red peppers, the colors form a palette of spring.

vegetable oil

1 Spanish onion, diced

1 teaspoon minced shallots

1 clove of garlic, minced

pinch saffron

3 cups chicken stock

2 potatoes, peeled and diced

salt to taste

1. In a heavy-bottomed saucepot, brown the onions, garlic and shallots in a little vegetable oil.

2 Add the saffron and diced potatoes, and the chicken stock.

3. Allow the mix to simmer for about 20 minutes, until the potatoes are soft.

4. Purée the mix in a blender.

5. If it is too thick, add additional stock. Serve with fish or chicken.

PESTO

At the end of summer, when the fields are full of more basil than you can possibly enjoy fresh in salads, it's time to make pesto. Pesto is a purée of basil in olive oil, with garlic, Parmesan and pine nuts, which is delicious on pasta, fish, poultry or sandwiches. It's not difficult to make. Use the best olive oil you can, it really makes a difference. Real pine nuts also make a big difference and are also expensive, but don't try to substitute walnuts. A blender will yield a much smoother purée than a food processor. Pesto will last for months in the refrigerator, and when it's cold and blustery outside, a dinner made with your own pesto will provide a memory of summer.

1. Remove the stems of the basil and discard them. Wash the leaves well and spin dry.

2. Place the basil, garlic and pine nuts in the blender in batches, and purée with olive oil.

3. In a large mixing bowl, add the grated cheese, lemon juice, vinegar and salt and pepper to the basil purée, and mix well.

4. Store in the refrigerator, and take out a little at a time as needed.

1 pound basil leaves

1 cup pine nuts

1 cup olive oil

6 cloves garlic

½ cup grated Parmesan cheese

juice of 1 lemon

2 tablespoons balsamic vinegar

salt and pepper

ROASTED PEPPER TAPENADE
Serves 8-10

Tapenade is a Mediterranean purée of olives, which is eaten with fish, chicken or even just bread. The intense flavor of the olives gives it a strong taste. The following recipe is for a tapenade made with olives and roasted peppers, among other things, which is flavorful and colorful, and prefect for the grilling season. It keeps for several days, and so if you are expecting a houseful of guests for the weekend, it can be put on grilled swordfish, tuna or poultry to make a quick and delicious meal.

1 roasted red pepper

½ cup reconstituted sun-dried tomatoes

½ cup pitted Greek olives

½ red onion, finely diced

1 bunch scallions, minced

½ teaspoon minced garlic

1 tablespoon minced parsley

½ teaspoon chopped fresh thyme

1 cup olive oil

½ cup balsamic vinegar

salt and pepper

1. Peel the roasted pepper, remove the seeds, and dice into small pieces.

2. Drain the dried tomatoes and dice finely.

3. Dice the olives into small pieces.

4. In a stainless bowl, combine together all the ingredients and mix well. Taste for salt and pepper, and either serve immediately or refrigerate for several days.

TOMATO BASIL SALSA
Serves 4

There are only a few short weeks when we can enjoy a really ripe and delicious tomato, so when that season is upon us, it behooves us to eat as many of them as we can. And for those who love tomatoes, there aren't enough ways to eat them. The following recipe for tomato basil salsa is delicious on grilled fish or chicken, or for spreading on bread. Be sure to use only the ripest tomatoes.

1. Toast the pine nuts in a small skillet over medium heat. Place the nuts directly in the pan without any oil, and shake vigorously for 2-3 minutes until brown. Set aside and cool.

2. Remove the core from the tomatoes and drop in boiling water for 30 seconds. Remove from the pot and plunge in ice water.

3. Peel the skin off the tomatoes, remove the seeds, and chop coarsely with a large knife.

4. In a small stainless bowl, mix the tomatoes together with the remaining ingredients, including the toasted nuts, and serve on grilled fish.

3 tablespoons pine nuts

3 large ripe tomatoes

ice water bath

½ small red onion, finely diced

1 bunch scallion, minced

2 tablespoons minced chopped basil

1 teaspoon minced garlic

3 tablespoons olive oil

2 tablespoons balsamic vinegar

freshly ground pepper

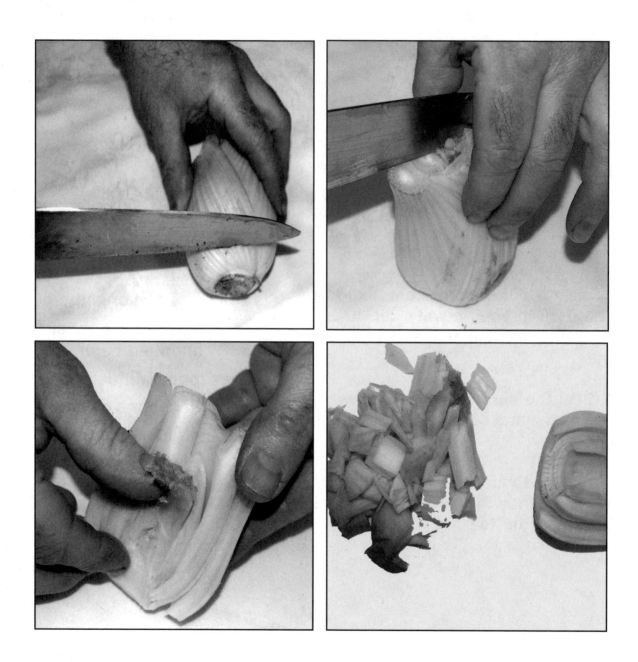

FENNEL AND PERNOD SAUCE

For 4 servings of fish

One of the great food affinities is between tomatoes and fennel, and fish. This is the seasoning basis of bouillabaisse, the classic Mediterranean fish soup, which includes these ingredients. But making fish soup is a complicated business, which requires many different seafood ingredients, and is expensive as well. However, it is possible to combine the flavors in a simpler way. You can easily prepare a sauce that combines fresh minced fennel braised with saffron, tomato and Pernod, which can be served with any hearty fish like bass or snapper. Pernod is the classic French anise-flavored liqueur. The anise flavor can be reinforced by also adding either fennel pollen, or finely ground fennel seeds. This sauce is considerably easier than making bouillabaisse, but provides much of the same flavor satisfaction.

1. Trim the fennel, cut in half, and remove the tough fibery center. Separate the leaves of the bulbs, and dice.

2 In a skillet or saucepot heat a little olive oil, and lightly brown the shallots. Add the fresh fennel, saffron, garlic, ground fennel seeds, tomatoes and wine, and simmer slowly for about 5 minutes until the fennel is soft.

3. Add a splash of Pernod, and serve with broiled, baked or grilled fish.

1 head fennel

olive oil

1 tablespoon minced shallot

½ cup peeled diced tomatoes

pinch saffron

¼ cup white wine

¼ teaspoon minced garlic

pinch fennel pollen or ground fennel seeds

splash Pernod

181

ROASTED GARLIC SAUCE
Serves 4-6

When used raw, garlic is essential in most of the world's great cuisines, from French and Italian to Chinese and Thai. But when roasted at a low temperature garlic mellows and takes on a very different character. The key to roasting garlic is that it be done at a very low temperature, otherwise it burns and develops a bitter flavor. The roasted cloves can be spread on croutons or bread and enjoyed that way, but they can also be used to make a delicious sauce. The following recipe for roasted garlic sauce can be enjoyed with any grilled or roasted meat, including pork tenderloin.

1 whole head of garlic

drizzle olive oil

pinch fresh thyme

1½ cups veal or chicken stock

1. Set the oven to its lowest temperature setting, about 150°-175°

2. Place the whole head of garlic flat side on the counter, and smash the top with a skillet to separate the cloves. Drizzle with a little olive oil and fresh thyme and bake for about 1 hour, or until soft.

3. Remove the roasted garlic from the oven, peel away the remaining papery skin and discard.

4. Place the stock in a small saucepot, add the garlic and simmer for about 5 minutes.

5. Purée the stock and roasted garlic cloves in a blender.

6. Serve with roasted or grilled meats.

The summer season is the time to eat cold poached salmon, and the classic accompaniment is a green herb-flavored mayonnaise known as sauce vert. In fact, the same sauce is delicious on hot or grilled fish. The technique involves puréeing some fresh herbs in a blender with a little vegetable oil. Which herbs you use is somewhat up to you, and a blend of several is delicious. Some combination of fresh tarragon, dill, and basil works well, and parsley and some capers can also be added to the mix. Fresh herbs are essential. Don't try to make this with the dry variety. When blended with some homemade or purchased mayonnaise, the sauce is a quick and easy to make, and colorful as well.

1. Wash the herbs well, and purée with the capers in a blender with the vegetable oil.

2. Place the mayonnaise in a small mixing bowl, and slowly whisk in the herb purée, adding just a little at a time, and mixing well after each addition.

3. The sauce can be used to cover the bottom of the plate to create a beautiful green background to place fish on top of, or it can be put into a squeeze bottle and drizzled on top of grilled fish.

½ bunch dill

½ bunch fresh basil

2 sprigs tarragon

1 tablespoon capers

¾ cup vegetable oil

2 cups mayonnaise

CHICKEN STOCK
Makes 3 quarts

In the heart of winter, when the common cold is rampant, it's time to prepare that timeless cure-all—chicken stock. When someone advises eating a little chicken soup to help make you feel better, they're not talking about opening up a can. Nothing could be simpler to prepare. Just cover some chicken bones with cold water, add some carrot, celery, and onion, and let simmer. Never add salt to stock. Stock lasts for at least 5 days in the refrigerator, and can be frozen. The word in French for stock is fond, as in foundation, and stock is indeed the foundation of classic French cooking. It can be used in soups, in braised dishes, or just eaten alone as broth.

5 pounds chicken bones

1 onion, peeled and sliced

½ head celery, chopped

2 carrots, chopped

2 bay leaves

½ teaspoon whole black peppercorns

1 tablespoon dry thyme

1. Rinse the bones well, to remove any blood.

2. Place the bones in a heavy-bottomed pot and add the chopped vegetables and herbs.

3. Fill the pot with cold water, and bring to a boil.

4. Allow to simmer at low heat for about 1 hour. Use a ladle to skim off any foam or fat that rises to the surface.

5. Pour the liquid through a strainer, and discard the bones.

6. Use the stock for soup or sauces.

VEAL STOCK

Makes about 1 gallon of stock, or 2 quarts of demi-glacé

While not difficult to make, it is time consuming, and takes up a lot of space on the stove, and it is generally something made only by restaurant kitchens. One way to distinguish a high quality and serious continental restaurant is if the chef makes real veal stock. In a good restaurant, if you have ever had a rich brown sauce on beef, veal, poultry, or even fish, it may well have been made with veal stock. Onion soup, steak au poivre, veal scaloppini and coq au vin are made with veal stock. When the basic stock is reduced by half, it is known as demi-glacé, because it is much more concentrated in flavor.

1. Preheat the oven to 325°

2. In a heavy-bottomed roasting pan, roast the bones for 2 hours.

10 pounds veal bones

3. Remove the bones from the oven, and place them in a large heavy-bottomed sauce pot.

2 cups tomato paste

4. Add the tomato paste, chopped vegetables, and spices.

2 onions, chopped

2 carrots, chopped

5. Cover the bones with cold water and bring to a boil on top of the stove. Mix in the tomato paste so it dissolves, and then turn the flame down to a low simmer. Cook on a low flame for 8-12 hours.

½ head of celery, chopped

2 bay leaves

6. Remove the bones from the pot, and pass the liquid through a strainer.

½ teaspoon black peppercorns

7. Bring the strained stock to a boil, and remove any grease that rises to the top.

pinch thyme

8. You can use this as stock in braised dishes, or use it in sauces by reducing the liquid by half.

CASTLE STREET
DIJON VINAIGRETTE

There is no reason to use commercially prepared dressings, which often contain preservatives and chemicals, when making your own is so easy. I prefer soybean or vegetable oil for the clear, neutral taste. A strong olive oil can be overpowering. The key to the following recipe is to add the oil slowly, whisking the dressing well as you do.

3 cups soybean oil

1 cup red wine vinegar

1½ tablespoons
Dijon mustard

1 tablespoon minced shallot

1 egg yolk

salt and pepper to taste

1. Combine the egg yolk, mustard, shallot, and ⅓ cup of vinegar in a mixing bowl. Whisk together well.

2. Slowly add in the oil, alternating it with the remaining vinegar, just a little bit at a time, whisking well before each additon of oil. If you add the oil too quickly, the dressing will break.

3. Season with salt and pepper. Store refrigerated.

DESSERTS

Fruit tarts traditionally involve a pastry shell, but in this instance the cored out pineapple ring functions as the tart shell. This is simpler to make, has fewer calories, and makes a refreshingly light and colorful warm-weather dessert. The variety of golden pineapples from Costa Rica are consistently sweet and juicy, and vastly superior to varieties previously found in the market. You can either buy prepared fruit purées for the sauces, or easily prepare them yourself by puréeing the fruit with a little sugar in a blender. This recipe involves assembling, not baking, and is a perfect for pastry novices.

1. Cut off the top and bottom of a ripe pineapple and trim away all the skin from the outside.

2. Cut the pineapple into ½"-¾" discs.

3. Use a thin paring knife to cut around the core of the pineapple, and remove the core entirely.

4. Place a pineapple ring on each of 6 plates. Fill the center of the pineapple ring with assorted fresh berries, and scatter some berries around the perimeter of the plate. Drizzle some of each of the raspberry sauce and mango sauce over the plate, and serve.

1 pineapple

2 pints blueberries

2 pints raspberries

1 pint strawberries

1 cup raspberry sauce or purée

1 cup mango sauce or purée

CARAMELIZED BANANAS WITH TWO SAUCES

Serves 4

One of the great comfort foods is warm bananas, and a little bit of brandy, sugar and cinnamon in a pan go a long way to transform this ordinary fruit into a delicious dessert. Chocolate sauce is quite simple to make, but caramel requires a little more work. Together they form a wonderful combination that can be decoratively drizzled on a dessert plate with the use of squeeze bottles. On a cool night they make for a great end to a meal.

Chocolate sauce:

4 ounces bitter-sweet chocolate

2 ounces heavy cream

Caramel sauce:

4 ounces sugar

2 ounces heavy cream

Caramelized bananas:

2 bananas

2 ounces brown sugar

dash cinnamon

1 tablespoon butter

splash brandy

1. To make the chocolate sauce, melt the chocolate and the cream together in a double boiler, and set aside.

2. To make the caramel, place the sugar in a skillet, and cook over moderate to high heat until the sugar begins to melt. As the sugar turns light brown, stir with a wooden spoon. When the sugar is completely dissolved, add the cream and continue to cook until the mix is completely liquefied. Set aside and keep warm.

3. Peel and dice the bananas. Heat the butter in a skillet, and add the bananas, brown sugar and cinnamon. Toss for a minute, add the brandy with care, and cook until the flames subside.

4. Scoop a little of your favorite ice cream onto the center of a dessert plate. Spoon the warm bananas around the perimeter of the plate. Drizzle some of each of the chocolate and caramel sauces on top and serve immediately.

CHOCOLATE HAZELNUT TERRINE
Serves 8

The period between Valentine's Day and Easter is the height of chocolate season, when so many of us eat and buy chocolate. One of the classic combinations is chocolate and hazelnut, which is characteristic of Austria. The key to this dessert is good quality hazelnut paste, which is like a sweetened version of peanut butter, except made from hazelnuts. The terrine needs to be chilled to firm up, but is best eaten at room temperature. The result is a rich, dense but creamy slab that should satisfy the most sophisticated chocophile.

1. Lightly grease a 4 x 4 inch mold.

2. Melt the chocolate over a double boiler with the Frangelico.

3. In an electric mixer, beat the butter and sugar together until soft.

4. Combine the melted chocolate and butter mix, and stir well.

5. Add the hazelnut paste, and mix well. Pour into the mold.

6. Chill for several hours. Run under hot water to unmold the terrine, and serve at room temperature with Crème Anglaise or chocolate sauce.

1 pound bitter-sweet chocolate

16 ounces hazelnut paste

6 ounces confectioner's sugar

8 ounces unsalted butter

1 tablespoon Frangelico liqueur

WARM APPLE PANCAKE WITH VANILLA ICE CREAM
Makes about 4 pancakes

Autumn turns our thoughts to apples, and warm desserts. In a variation on the traditional potato pancake, I thought of the idea of making a sweetened apple pancake made from grated apples, and the result is a delicious warm pancake, perfect for helping vanilla ice cream melt on top. There is very little flour in the recipe, and the bulk of the pancake is simply grated apples. You must fry these pancake up immediately after grating the apples or they will turn brown. A drizzle of maple syrup on top completes the dish.

3 Granny Smith apples

¼ cup confectioner's sugar

2 eggs

¼ cup flour

½ teaspoon grated ginger

dash cinnamon

dash nutmeg

¼ cup raisins

1. Peel the apples. Grate them with a 4-sided hand grater.

2. Combine all the remaining ingredients in a mixing bowl, and mix well.

3. Form into 4 equal-sized pancakes.

4. In a hot skillet, fry the pancakes in hot vegetable oil for about 1 minute on each side. Top with vanilla ice cream, and drizzle with maple syrup.

FROZEN LEMON SOUFFLÉ

The torrid heat of summer calls for desserts that don't require baking. And while during the colder months of the year dessert frequently means chocolate, in the summer the lighter flavors of fruit are more appropriate. Making a frozen soufflé is a lot easier than making a hot dessert soufflé. For starters, they must be prepared in advance, and you don't have to worry if your soufflé is going to rise properly. The key to beating egg whites is to make sure they are warm, which isn't a problem this time of year. A springform pan makes it easy to remove and serve. A drizzle of raspberry purée is all that's needed to complete this dessert.

1. Beat the cream into soft peaks, and set aside in the refrigerator.

2. Beat the yolks well with the sugar, and add the lemon juice and zest.

3. Beat the warm egg whites in a mixer until light and frothy.

4. Fold the whites into the lemon-yolk mixture.

5. Fold the whipped cream into the mix.

6. Pour into a springform pan, and freeze overnight.

7. Unmold, and serve with raspberry purée.

3 cups heavy cream

8 eggs, separated

2 cups sugar

1 cup freshly squeezed lemon juice

grated zest of 2 lemons

LEMON ROULADE
Serves 8

A simple and light spring dessert is a lemon roulade filled with a lemon cream. The technique involves making the classic French cake known as génoise, which involves folding flour and melted butter into frothy, well-beaten eggs. The filling is made by adding lemon juice and grated lemon zest to whipped cream. One trick to helping whipped cream stay firm is to add a little unflavored gelatin to the whipped cream, which prevents the cream from breaking down. Serve with a drizzle of raspberry sauce for a light but satisfying dessert.

Cake:
6 eggs

6 ounces sugar

grated zest of 2 lemons

6 ounces flour

3 ounces melted butter

Filling:
2 pints whipping cream

2 sheets or packages unflavored gelatin

grated zest and juice of 2 lemons

1½ cups confectioner's sugar

parchment paper

1. Preheat oven to 350°

2. To make the cake, line a 16" x 12" sheet pan with parchment paper.

3. Combine the eggs, sugar and grated lemon zest in the bowl of an electric mixer, and warm over a burner until the eggs are warm to the touch.

4. Beat at high speed for about 4 minutes, until the batter has tripled in volume.

5. Slowly fold in the flour, alternating with the melted butter.

6. Bake for about 7-9 minutes, or until a toothpick inserted into the cake comes out clean. Allow cake to cool.

7. Place another sheet of parchment paper over the top of the cake, and using another pan, invert the cake, and remove it, leaving the bottom of the cake with the cooked parchment paper topside.

8. To make the filling, dissolve the gelatin in cold water, and set aside.

9. Whip the cream until almost stiff, add the sugar and grated zest, and whip a little more.

10. Heat the dissolved gelatin over low heat until it liquefies, and then add it to the whipped cream, and add the lemon juice.

11. Use about half the lemon cream to lightly frost ¾ of the surface of the cake.

12. Use the parchment paper to assist in rolling up the sheet into a jellyroll. Use the remaining cream to frost the top of the cake.

13. Chill the cake. To serve, slice thinly, and serve with raspberry sauce.

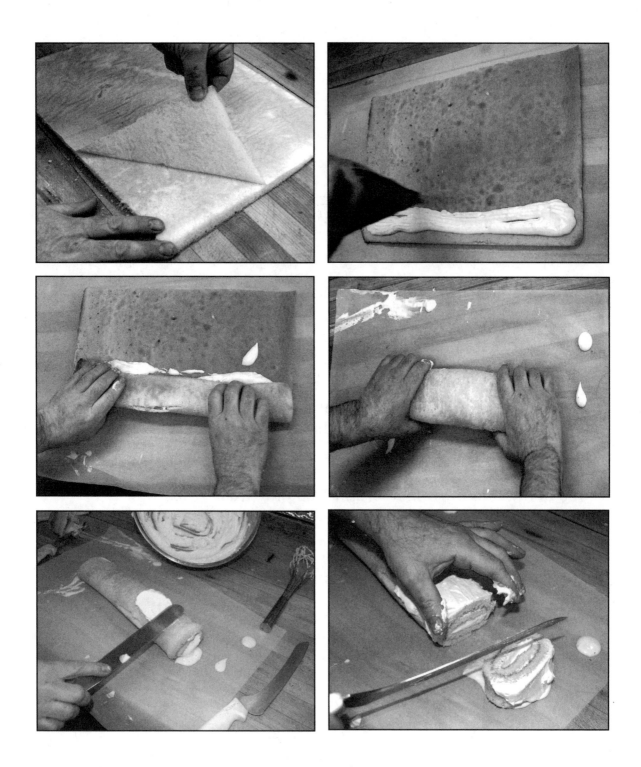

FLOURLESS CHOCOLATE MOUSSE CAKE

Serves 8

The notion of a flourless cake is hard to grasp for some, but this cake will make a believer out of the most die-hard skeptic. It is not difficult to make, but there are a few keys to success. High quality chocolate is absolutely essential, and some good quality European brands include Callebaut and Valrohna. The cake is easier to remove from the pan when chilled, but tastes best when at room temperature. Make sure the eggs are very warm before beating.

1. Preheat oven to 300°

2. Butter and flour a bread pan, and line with parchment paper.

3. Whip the cream, and set aside in the refrigerator.

4. Combine the hot coffee, rum, vanilla and melt the chocolate in it in a double boiler

5. Combine the eggs and sugar in an electric mixing bowl. Warm the egg mixture over a low flame on the stove until the eggs are warm to the touch. Beat the eggs at high speed for 5 minutes, until they have tripled in volume.

6. Fold the melted chocolate into the eggs.

7. Fold in the whipped cream.

8. Pour the mix into the loaf pan, and place pan in a water bath. Bake for 1 hour.

9. Let cool before inverting pan to remove cake. Serve at room temperature.

Ingredients:

flour

butter

parchment paper

1 cup heavy cream

12 ounces bittersweet chocolate

1 teaspoon vanilla

1 teaspoon dark rum

½ cup strong coffee

6 eggs

½ cup sugar

APPLE SPICE CAKE
Serves 8

A key part of autumn cuisine involves apples. They are delicious eaten raw, baked in pies or made into sauce. The following recipe is easy to make, can be made in advance, and produces a very moist apple spice cake. The apples add both sweetness and moisture to the cake, and it's a great way to utilize slightly bruised apples. And because this cake uses vegetable oil instead of butter, it is much lower in fat than most cakes.

2 eggs

2 cups sugar

2 teaspoons baking soda

2 teaspoons cinnamon

½ teaspoon nutmeg

pinch salt

1 teaspoon vanilla

2 cups flour

4 cups peeled, diced Macintosh apples

1½ cup vegetable oil

1 cup walnuts

½ cup raisins

1. Preheat the oven to 350° Grease a 9" x 13" pan.

2. Cream the eggs and sugar.

3. Add the remaining ingredients, and mix well.

4. Bake about 50 minutes. Allow to cool before serving.

Those who who are willing to do the extra work of picking their own blueberries will be richly rewarded. The wild variety are smaller and perhaps tarter than the cultivated species, but the flavor is more intense, and the hike to the areas where they are found is part of the pleasure. The topping for cobblers is much easier to make than rolling out a crust for a pie, but the filling is similar. They should be eaten slightly warm, to help facilitate the melting of vanilla ice cream.

Filling:

3 pints blueberries

¾ cup water

3 tablespoons cornstarch

dash cinnamon

dash nutmeg

grated zest of 1 lemon

1¼ cups sugar

1. Preheat oven to 350°

2. Combine 2 pints of blueberries with the sugar, cold water, cornstarch and spices, and bring to a boil while stirring. The cornstarch will thicken the mix.

3. Purée the cooked berries briefly on "pulse" in a food processor.

4. In a mixing bowl, combine the cooked berries with the remaining pint of raw berries and mix well.

5. Pour the berry mix into individual ramekins, or into a shallow baking dish.

Topping:

¾ cup sugar

1 cup flour

1 tablespoon baking powder

1 egg

3 tablespoons melted butter

6. To make the topping, combine the sugar, flour and baking powder in a mixing bowl and mix in the egg. Stir well.

7. Loosely sprinkle the topping over the berries, and then drizzle the melted butter on top.

8. Bake 15 minutes and serve warm, with vanilla ice cream.

HONEY CAKE
Makes 2 small loaves

Sweet cakes and spice are part of the holiday tradition regardless of religion, and the prospect of company and entertaining brings out the baking in all of us. The following recipe for honey cake yields a moist dark cake, which isn't too sweet, and is perfect for breakfast or brunch as well as dessert. The coffee and honey in the cake make for a rich dark-colored loaf. Avoid baking this cake in a convection oven, which causes the cake to fall after coming out of the oven.

2 teaspoons baking soda

1 cup strong coffee

4 eggs

2 cups sugar

½ pound dark honey

2 teaspoons allspice

1½ teaspoons ground ginger

¼ teaspoon nutmeg

5 tablespoons vegetable oil

4 cups flour

2 teaspoons baking powder

½ cup chopped walnuts

½ cup raisins

parchment paper

1. Preheat oven to 325°

2. Dissolve baking soda in hot coffee.

3. Beat eggs and sugar, add honey and spices.

4. Combine flour and baking powder. Combine hot coffee mix and vegetable oil.

5. Alternate adding flour mixture and hot coffee mixture to the beaten eggs and sugar.

6. Add raisins and nuts.

7. Bake in a well-greased loaf pan lined with parchment. Place the loaf pan in a water bath and bake for 1 hour. Allow to cool well before unmolding.

COCONUT MACAROONS
Makes 12-18 cookies

Religious holidays are not usually times for culinary innovation, but rather a time to eat traditional foods passed down for generations. One such traditional food is coconut macaroons at Passover. Because of the restriction against the use of flour, most traditional cakes, cookies and pies cannot be served at this holiday. Macaroons, however, can be made without flour, using finely ground matzoh and well-beaten egg whites. A well-made macaroon should be so light and fluffy as to almost float off the plate. And they are so delicious you will want to make them any time of year.

1. Preheat oven to 325°

2. Mix together matzoh meal, salt and sugar.

3. Have egg whites at room temperature. Beat until stiff.

4. Fold the beaten whites into the matzoh meal mix. Add the vanilla.

5. Fold in the coconut.

6. Drop by spoonfuls onto a well-greased cookie sheet, or one lined with parchment paper. Bake 15-20 minutes, or until golden.

2 tablespoons matzoh meal

½ cup sugar

pinch salt

2 egg whites

½ teaspoon vanilla extract

2 cups shredded coconut

PISTACHIO BISCOTTI
Makes about 3

When the holiday season is upon us, and if you are alienated by the crass commercialism or overwhelmed by the prospect of shopping either online or in the malls, there is an alternative. Nothing shows you care like the gift of homemade baked goods. The last thing many people need is another book, CD, tie or sweater. Homemade cookies are a wonderful way to spread good cheer. There are many varieties of traditional Christmas cookies, but biscotti are one of my favorites. They have the additional advantage of aging well; they actually taste better after a week or two when they dry out a little than when freshly baked. In addition, they are easy to make in large quantities, so you can make several people's gifts at once. The following recipe for pistachio biscotti is not difficult to make, and they will be sure to bring joy to those who receive them.

½ pound butter

¾ cup sugar

½ cup brown sugar

4 eggs

¼ cup brandy

¼ cup fennel seeds

6 cups flour

1 teaspoon salt

1 teaspoon baking soda

2 teaspoons baking powder

1 cup shelled unsalted pistachios

juice and grated zest of 2 lemons

1. Preheat oven to 350°

2. Cream butter, sugars, and eggs.

3. Add remaining ingredients.

4. Form into loaves, like a meatloaf, and place on a greased baking pan.

5. Bake 25 minutes; the cookies are only partially done at this point.

6. Cool slightly, and using a serrated knife, slice into ½" strips, lay out on baking pan, and bake 15 more minutes until slightly golden. Remove from oven and let cool.

CHOCOLATE HAZELNUT DACQUOISE

Serves 8

As the holidays approach, we entertain more, and tend to eat a little more richly than we do at other times of the year. Dacquoise is a tort made from folding ground nuts into beaten egg whites, and the result is a chewy cookie cake. The following recipe is not difficult to make, though it does require some time to assemble, and calls for hazelnut paste, which is expensive and only available at gourmet shops. The result is a showstopper dessert that will impress your guests and family. Since it so rich, a small thin slice is all that is required.

1. Preheat oven to 300°

2. To make the cake, separate 6 eggs, warm the whites over a burner on the stove and beat at high speed in an electric mixer. Slowly add in the sugar and continue whipping until the whites are firm.

3. Carefully fold in the ground nuts and flour.

4. Pour onto an 8 x 8 inch sheet pan lined with parchment paper and bake for 30 minutes. Allow to cool.

5. When cool, remove the cake from the pan and cut into 3 evenly sized pieces.

Cake:

6 egg whites

1 cup sugar

1 cup finely ground almonds or hazelnuts

1 ounce flour

parchment paper

6. To make the hazelnut filling, beat the egg whites in the bowl of an electric mixer, and when they start to stiffen, slowly add the sugar.

7. Place the hazelnut paste in another bowl of an electric mixer, and the butter, and beat well. Fold the beaten egg whites into the hazelnut mix.

8. Spread the hazelnut mix over 2 of the 3 pieces of the cake, and assemble like making a 3-layered sandwich, leaving the top layer of the cake without the hazelnut filling.

9. To make the chocolate frosting, combine the chocolate and cream in a bowl in a double boiler, and melt over steam.

10. Pour the chocolate frosting over the top and sides of the assembled cake.

11. Allow the dacquoise to chill for at least 1 hour, and slice into thin pieces to serve.

Hazelnut cream:

2 egg whites

¼ cup sugar

¼ pound butter

1 cup hazel-nut paste

Chocolate frosting:

1 cup bitter-sweet chocolate

½ cup heavy cream

CHOCOLATE FUDGE COOKIES

Makes 3 dozen large cookies

The following recipe for chocolate fudge cookies is easy to make in large quantities, and the dough stores well in the refrigerator for weeks so you can bake off cookies gradually. There's something about cookies dusted in confectioners' sugar that is particularly appealing during the holiday season, as if they reflect the snowy weather outside. These cookies are at their best when lightly cooked and pleasantly moist and chewy; be careful not to overbake and dry them out too much.

2 ounces unsalted butter

4 ounces bitter-sweet chocolate

4 eggs

2 cups sugar

2 cups flour

2 tablespoons baking powder

1/4 teaspoon salt

1/2 cup walnuts

confectioners' sugar

1. Preheat oven to 350°

2. Melt the butter and chocolate together in a double boiler.

3. Cream together the eggs and sugar, and then alternate the chocolate mix with the rest of the dry ingredients (except for the confectioners' sugar) and mix well.

4. Chill the dough in the refrigerator for at least 2 hours.

5. Scoop or roll the dough into flattened balls, and then roll them in a generous quantity of confectioners' sugar until they are well coated and white.

6. Bake for about 5 minutes on a greased cookie sheet or pan lined with parchment paper. Allow to cool before trying to remove from the pan.

WARM BREAD PUDDING

Yields 6-8

Bread pudding is essentially a variation on the many desserts that are made from custard, like crème brulée, flan, and crème caramel. There is something about it that appeals to our primal desires and transports us back to childhood. Eggs are at the heart of these desserts, which must be baked carefully in a water bath at a low temperature to prevent the custard from curdling. It's a great way to recycle stale bread, and their transformation into a rich indulgent dessert is nothing short of remarkable.

1. Preheat oven to 300°

2. Melt the butter and use some of it to grease 8 ramekins.

3. Combine the bread chunks and the remaining melted butter in a small bowl and mix well with the currants.

4. In another small bowl, whisk the eggs, egg yolks and sugar together.

5. Combine the cream and milk together in a small saucepot and bring to a boil.

6. Add the milk mix to the beaten egg mix and whisk well.

7. Place the bread chunks in the ramekins.

8. Fill the ramekins with the custard mix.

9. Place in a water bath and bake for 20-25 minutes. Serve with Crème Anglaise (see page 208).

4 tablespoons butter

3 cups stale bread chunks

½ cup dried black currants

3 eggs

2 egg yolks

¾ cup sugar

1½ cups milk

1 cup cream

CRÈME ANGLAISE

Serves 6

1½ cups milk

4 egg yolks

½ cup sugar

½ teaspoon vanilla

¼ cup cream

rum or Gran Marnier (optional)

1. Bring milk to a boil. Set aside.

2. Separate eggs, and combine yolks, vanilla and sugar in a small bowl and whisk well.

3. Add hot milk to the yolk and sugar mixture and whisk well.

4. Place the heavy cream in another small bowl, which should be in an ice bath.

5. Place the bowl with yolk mixture directly on top of a burner on the stove over moderate heat and whisk well, continuing to stir until the sauce starts to thicken. Be careful not to overcook, or the eggs will scramble.

6. Pour the thickened sauce into the cream in the ice bath. This will help cool down the sauce.

7. If desired, add rum or Gran Marnier.

INDEX

A

acorn squash, stuffed, 42
almond crusted brook trout, 76
angel hair pasta:
>with asparagus and
>>parmesan, 60
>with sautéed shrimp, 95

apple spice cake, 198
apple walnut turkey stuffing, 124
apples:
>breast of duck and black
>>currants with, 115
>Granny Smith; in Asian
>>slaw, 44
>in slow-roasted vege-
>>tables, 49
>in stuffed acorn
>>squash, 42
>in stuffed pork loin, 128
>Macintosh, in stuffed
>>acorn squash, 42
>spice cake, 198
>walnut turkey stuffing, 124
>warm pancake with vanilla
>>ice cream, 192

artichoke vinaigrette, 36
arugula, walnut crusted salmon
>with, 77
asian slaw, 44
asparagus:
>angel hair pasta and, 60
>chilled, with sesame

>sauce, 53
>with fettuccini and shiitake
>>mushrooms, 68
>grilled, 52
>and sautéed salmon, 88
>and spinach timbale, 54
>white, with goat cheese
>>gratin, 34

B

bacon:
>with shad roe, 78
>lardons, in frisée salad, 30
>slab; with duck, 120
>>with pork tenderloin, 131
>>with sautéed kale, 40
>smoked, in three little pig
>>pasta, 69
>in Tuscan bean soup, 9

balsamic and rosemary
>marinated filet mignon, 138
balsamic vinaigrette, 27
barley, roasted, salad, 24
beans:
>black, soup, 4
>Tuscan, soup, 9
>fava, chicken with, 112

beets:
>with walnuts and endive, 20
>braised, with salmon, 92
Berkshire blue cheese, breast of
>chicken stuffed with, 108